W9-ANA-772

Our Debt to Greece and Rome

EDITORS
GEORGE DEPUE HADZSITS, PH.D.

DAVID MOORE ROBINSON, PH.D., LL.D.

PLATE I. EARTH AND SEA

From the Eastern Pediment of the Parthenon

LOVE OF NATURE AMONG THE GREEKS AND ROMANS

BY

HENRY RUSHTON FAIRCLOUGH

Professor of Classical Literature

COOPER SQUARE PUBLISHERS, INC.

NEW YORK

1963

Published 1963 by Cooper Square Publishers, Inc.
59 Fourth Avenue, New York 3, N. Y.
Library of Congress Catalog Card No. 63-10298

PRINTED IN THE UNITED STATES OF AMERICA

CONTENTS

ILLUSTRATIONS

LOVE OF NATURE AMONG THE GREEKS AND ROMANS

LOVE OF NATURE AMONG THE GREEKS AND ROMANS

I. PROLOGUE

A sympathy with the imaginings of old is the best incentive to an aesthetic estimate not only of art but of nature today.[1] CHARLES MILLS GAYLEY

Wife, dear is this light of the sun, and lovely to the eye is the placid ocean-flood, and the earth in the bloom of spring, and wide-spreading waters, and of many lovely sights might I speak the praises. But nought is so fair or lovely to behold, as for the childless and those consumed with longings, to see in their homes the light that new-born babes bring.[2] EURIPIDES

THE FEELING for nature among the ancients and the treatment of nature in Greek and Roman literature are subjects that have attracted a good deal of attention in the last quarter of a century.

The discussion, however, may be said to have begun as early as 1795 with the publication of Schiller's essay on "Naïve and Senti-

[1] *The Classic Myths in English Literature and in Art,* Introduction, p. xxxii.
[2] Frag. 316, Ed. Nauck.

mental Poetry." Schiller draws a sharp distinction between the simple poetry of the ancients and the sentimental poetry of modern times, remarking that " we find very few traces in Greek poetry of the sentimental interest with which the modern world looks upon scenes of nature and natural characters. The Greeks, to be sure, are accurate and faithful in their descriptions of nature, but they show no more peculiar enthusiasm than in describing a vestment, a shield, armor, a piece of furniture or any mechanical product. . . They do not cling to nature with the emotion, spirituality or gentle melancholy of the moderns."

This somewhat narrow view of Schiller's is to be explained by the fact that he was most familiar with Homer, the most naïve of all poets. Later, in his criticism of Matthison's poems, Schiller admitted that the Greeks were susceptible to the charm of inanimate nature, their very mythology indicating how deep and rich was their appreciation. Even in his " Naïve and Sentimental Poetry " Schiller had recognized certain poets, such as Euripides, Horace, Propertius, Virgil, and Ovid, as the sentimental poets of antiquity, but any modifications of his first sweeping statement were forgotten, and Schiller is probably responsible for the wide-spread view, that the Greeks and Romans totally failed to appreciate the beauty and picturesqueness of the external world.

Thus Becker in his *Charicles* says: "No author of the better age has even attempted to portray a landscape. . . The Greeks wanted that deep and warm perception of the charms of inanimate nature, the lack of which, when found among us, is always a cause of reproach or commiseration"; and Otfried Müller assures us that "neither the sentimental dwelling upon nature in general, nor the romantic conception of landscape in particular, is known to the Greek spirit." The same view was emphatically expressed by Cope in an essay on "The Picturesque among the Greeks."[3]

The first to contradict this view was Jacobs, in 1824. "Who," he asks, "would regard the pictures of nature and her phenomena, which Homer has woven into the web of his epic, inferior to the lengthy descriptions of those who have devoted their energy exclusively to depicting nature? Even the *Anthology* is not poor in poems which glorify her charms, and invite the reader to the shade of rustling plane-

[3] E. M. Cope, *Cambridge Essays,* London, 1856.

trees, on the edge of murmuring brooks or in cool meadows."

According to Alexander von Humboldt, the Greek possessed a deep feeling for nature, but lacked the active consciousness which prompts men to express that feeling in words. Moreover, he tells us that though "in Greek antiquity we find the tenderest expressions of deep feeling for nature mingled with poetical presentations of human passion; yet such descriptions of nature are merely secondary, because in Greek art everything, so to speak, moves in the circle of human life. Nature-poetry, as a special branch of literature, was wholly foreign to the Greeks; landscape with them appears only as the background of a picture, in front of which move human forms." The principle here set forth is well illustrated by the passage from Euripides cited above.

Heinrich Motz champions the simplicity, honesty and clearness of vision possessed by the ancients, and ridicules the affected sentiment, the *enthousiasme obligé* of the moderns. Friedländer, however, is wiser in his discrimination, and expresses the view that among the ancients the feeling for nature, while vivid, sincere and deep, was much more limited in its range than among the moderns, being confined to a sentiment for what is lovely and charming to the eye. He maintains that an appreciation of the wild and sublime in nature is quite foreign to both antiquity and the middle ages.

More recent writers upon this subject have followed the historical method, and have found among the ancients themselves a process of development in their appreciation of nature, corresponding to their intellectual and social development. This idea Alfred Biese sets forth in his *Development of the Feeling for Nature,* among the Greeks (Vol. I), the Romans (Vol. II), and in the Middle Ages and Modern times (Vol. III). The volume dealing with Greece devotes one chapter to the naïve feeling for nature in mythology and Homer, a second to the sympathetic feeling in lyric poetry and the drama, and a third to the sentimental and idyllic feeling in Hellenistic and imperial times.

Following upon Biese's work appeared an essay on "The Dawn of Romanticism in Greek Poetry" by Professor Butcher, given in his book *Some Aspects of the Greek Genius.* The line of thought which he follows may be indicated by one of his opening paragraphs:

"The great change which passed over imaginative literature under the influence of Christianity was not without preparation. Within the limits of Greek literature itself there are many premonitory symptoms of the new direction in which feeling was tending, of a new attitude towards the things of the heart and another mode of contemplating the universe without. An exclusive attention to the earlier epochs of Greek literature has obscured the gradual stages of this process." The claim which Professor Butcher first made that this "change of sentiment sets in only from the time of Alexander onward" he rightly modified in his third edition (1904), where he admits that "there are many premonitions in Euripides." The present writer had published in 1897 an essay on "The Attitude of the Greek Tragedians Toward Nature," in which he endeavored to show how a love of nature, more or less latent in Aeschylus and Sophocles, becomes a conspicuous feature of Euripides, in whom it finds very definite expression. Euripides indeed may well be looked upon as the first of the Greek romanticists.

Since the opening of the present century numerous writers, many of whom will be cited in the course of this book, have dealt more or less fully with this subject, and as a result no one who has considered the evidence available would to-day venture to deny that the ancients had a very profound love of nature, which is indicated in various ways at various times, and which, when properly understood, is found to be quite as genuine and significant as any that has been voiced by the most ardent nature-lovers among our poets of the present day.

II. MYTHOLOGY AND RELIGION

Hail, lady, whoever of the blessed ones you are that are come to this house, whether Artemis, or Leto, or goddess Aphrodite, or high-born Themis, or bright-eyed Athene. Or, maybe, you are one of the Graces come hither, who bear the gods company and are called immortal, or also one of the Nymphs who haunt the pleasant woods, or of those who inhabit this lovely mountain and the springs of rivers and grassy woods. I will make you an altar upon a high peak in a far-seen place, and will sacrifice rich offerings to you at all seasons.[1]

HOMERIC HYMN TO APHRODITE

" Did you hear the guide say that the natives consider this to be the abode of gods? " And so saying, he lifted up his eyes to the mountain top.[2] PHILOSTRATUS

For the consciousness of the Greek, dead nature did not exist; all nature was life, spirit, divinity.[3] ZIELINSKI

There was a time when meadow, grove and stream,
The earth, and every common sight,
To me did seem
Apparelled in celestial light,
The glory and the freshness of a dream.

WORDSWORTH

You remember that in distinguishing Imagination from Idolatry, I referred you to the forms of passionate affection

[1] Translation, vss. 90 ff., by H. G. Evelyn-White, *Hesiod, The Homeric Hymns and Homerica,* in *The Loeb Classical Library,* 1914.

[2] Philostratus, *In Honour of Apollonius of Tyana,* II.5, tr. by J. S. Phillimore, 2 vols., Oxford, 1912.

[3] *The Religion of Ancient Greece;* tr. by G. R. Noyes, p. 15.

with which a noble people commonly regards the rivers and springs of its native land. Some conception of personality, or of spiritual power in the stream, is almost necessarily involved in such emotion.[4] RUSKIN

> Thou kingly Spirit throned among the hills,
> Thou dread ambassador from Earth to Heaven,
> Great hierarch! tell thou the silent sky
> And tell the stars, and tell yon rising sun,
> Earth, with her thousand voices, praises God.[5]

COLERIDGE

As they were watching the sea, he said with his queer smile: " It almost makes one believe her theory, that the old gods are not dead. Do you ever see them, Babs; or are you like me, obtuse? " Certainly about those lithe invasions of the sea-nymph waves, with ashy, streaming hair, flinging themselves into the arms of the land, there was the old pagan rapture, an inexhaustible delight, a passionate soft acceptance of eternal fate, a wonderful acquiescence in the untiring mystery of life.[6]

JOHN GALSWORTHY

Swinburne's " vision of nature is not that of a modern, but that of an early Greek poet. Such a poet as Wordsworth, who seeks sermons in stone, has another view of nature than that of the speaker of this poem, who calls on 'the gods hard by.' Which comes nearer to the great heart of nature? "[7]

There is a passage of singular eloquence in Mr. Conrad's *Mirror of the Sea* . . . 'The King of the West . . . is a barbarian of a northern type. Violent without craftiness, and furious without malice, one may imagine him seated masterfully, with a double-edged sword on his knees, upon

[4] *Aratra Pentelici,* 88.
[5] *Hymn Before Sunrise.*
[6] *The Patrician.*
[7] Theodore Wratislaw in *Algernon Charles Swinburne,* p. 144. He is speaking of *A Nympholept.*

the painted and gilt clouds of the sunset, bowing his shock head of golden locks, a flaming brand over his breast, imposing, colossal, mighty-limbed, with a thundering voice. . . . 'The other, the East King, the king of blood-red sunrises, with clear-cut features, black-browed and dark-eyed, grey-robed, upright in sunshine, resting a smooth-shaven cheek in the palm of his hand, impenetrable, secret, full of wiles, fine-drawn, keen-meditating aggressions.' [8]

THAT THE Greeks possessed a wonderful appreciation of the charm and picturesqueness of nature is really proved once for all by the character of their religion and the extraordinary richness and beauty of their mythology. Greek religion reveals a consciousness of the mystery of nature, "a consciousness not only of life, but of life infused with spirit: and not only with spirit, but with divinity. . . Nature was divine not only in its meadows and forests, in its springs and rivers, but equally divine in the measureless, surging expanse of its seas and in the silent immobility of its mountain wastes." [9] When the Greek viewed a rapid torrent, a grove of trees or a line of high cliffs, his imagination saw behind these objects an animate, divine

[8] Philip Guedalla, *Masters and Men,* London, 1923, p. 138. Homer's and Virgil's pictures of Aeolus and the Winds must have appealed strongly to Conrad.

[9] Zielinski, *The Religion of Ancient Greece,* p. 15.

spirit, though the river itself, the grove and the cliffs are to us nothing but dead inanimate bodies. He therefore bestowed the love and worship, which we moderns are wont to give to nature herself, not upon the lifeless bodies of material things, but upon the spiritual powers which made them their homes. Thus the very forms with which Greek fancy peopled rivers, woods and mountains, testify plainly to the emotions, the admiration and veneration aroused by the many phenomena of natural objects and forces.

No one has pointed out the beauty and spirituality of Greek religion more clearly than Zielinski. "Out of the earth, from a crevice in the rocks, gushes a cool spring, creating green life around it and quenching the thirst of the flocks and of their shepherd: this is a goddess, a nymph, a naiad. Let us thank her for her good will by good will, let us shelter her current with a roof, let us hollow out a basin beneath her, in order that in its gleaming surface she may contemplate her divine form. On appointed days let us not forget to cast her a wreath of field flowers, and to redden the bright waters with the blood of a lamb slain in her honor. On the other hand, if we come to her in time of doubt and anguish of spirit and incline our ears to her murmur, she will remember us and will whisper to us salutary counsel or a word of comfort. And if the place where she draws her bright waters is suited to human habitation, a city may arise there, and a whole people will worship her, all Hellas will glorify her. Such is Callirrhoë in Athens, Dirce in Thebes, Pirene in Corinth. Each morning the girls of the city will gather at the Naiad's sanctuary, in order to fill their jars with her water and to delight her kindly ears with girlish prattle, and in her purifying waters the inhabitants of the city will bathe their new-born children." [10]

Thus it is that the Greeks personified the various aspects of nature. Thus, in the truest sense of the word, they were the *imagists* of antiquity, or, as Jane Harrison calls them, *iconists,* for "in Greek mythology we have enshrined the images fashioned by the most gifted people the world has ever seen." [11]

As to the Romans, Miss Harrison assures us that, in contrast with the Greeks, they were never iconists, or image-makers: "they did not personify, did not create personalities,

[10] *Op. cit.,* pp. 17 ff. [11] *Mythology,* p. xiv.

hence they could not tell stories about persons, could not create *myths;* they had little or no mythology."

This is not quite true. To be sure the Romans were by nature far less imaginative than the Greeks, and their native mythology is far less personal, concrete and attractive than that of their neighbors and subjects. But the more the Romans came under the influence of Greece, the more fully did they make Greek thought and fancy their very own. Their fundamental ideas on nature, moreover, are largely the same and the Romans soon learned to look through Greek eyes. Not seldom, therefore, in their expression of a love for nature, the Roman poets write in purely Greek terms. Yet the sentiment for nature shown by Lucretius, Virgil, and all the other great Roman poets is thoroughly genuine, especially as the Italians themselves possessed a native warmth of feeling that no merely conventional forms of expression could serve to check. Ruskin finds in Horace's *fies nobilium tu quoque fontium* an "endearing and tender promise," and in Virgil's

te, Lari maxume, teque
Fluctibus et fremitu assurgens, Benaco, marino

a "joyful and proud affection" for "the lakes of his enchanted land." [12]

The most obvious illustration of the ancient personification of natural forces is to be found in the mutual love of Heaven and Earth, of Father Zeus or Jupiter, the sky-god, and Gaia or Terra, the Mother Earth. This idea runs from first to last through Greek and Roman literature. It is humanized, so to speak, in the union of Zeus and Hera in the *Iliad,* when "the divine earth sent forth new grass and dewy lotus, crocus and hyacinth," [13] — a passage described by Leaf as the most romantic in the epic — but perhaps the most familiar expression of the same idea occurs in Virgil's *Georgics:* [14] "Then Heaven, the Father almighty, comes down in fruitful showers into the lap of his joyous spouse, and his might, with her mighty frame commingling, nurtures all growths." The love that thus unites the Sky-father and the Earth-mother is, according to Aeschylus, no other than Aphrodite, whose universal power is seen in the marriage of heaven and earth, in the fertilizing rains, and in the birth of flocks of sheep and

[12] Ruskin, *Aratra Pentelici,* 88.
[13] *Iliad,* XIV, 341 ff.
[14] II. 325 ff.

the grain of the fields, as well as in the growth of trees.[15]

The famous invocation of Venus, which opens the great poem "On Nature" by Lucretius, conveys the same idea in a passage of singular beauty: "Mother of the Roman race, delight of gods and men, benign Venus, who under the gliding constellations of heaven fillest with thy presence the sea with its ships and the earth with its fruits, seeing that by thy power all the races of living things are conceived and come to being in the light of day, before thee O goddess the winds take flight, and the clouds of heaven at thy coming, at thy feet the brown earth sheds her flowers of a thousand hues, before thee the sea breaks into rippling laughter, and the untroubled sky glows with radiant light."[16]

If the sky is divine, so also are the great and imposing inhabitants thereof. And chief among these are the sun and moon. Nobody needs to be reminded of the beautiful myths in which the personality of these great bodies is set forth in Greek and Roman poetry. In all literatures indeed, ancient and modern, the sun

[15] Aeschylus, Fragment 44.
[16] Lucretius, I. 1 ff., as translated by C. H. Herford, in *The Poetry of Lucretius*, Manchester, 1918, p. 22.

and the moon are living powers, and in our own attitude toward them we are often not far removed from primitive man. The American geologist, Raphael Pumpelly, for example, can thus speak of the sun on the great table-land of Central Asia. "Often on this journey, in travelling northward, facing the strong Arctic winds, with a thermometer at 10° and 20° F. below zero, while almost ready to drop from the saddle, owing to stiffness from cold, I have turned my horse to face the sun, and have felt in a few minutes the warmth of its rays stealing gently through my veins like an influx of new vigor. . . How often have I then felt that, had I been born a nomad, I should have fallen down to worship the great light-giving god of day, as did the earliest bards, the authors of the Vedas.[17] Addison in his famous hymn,

> "*The spacious firmament on high*
> *With all the blue ethereal sky,*
> *And spangled heavens, a shining frame,*
> *Their great Original proclaim,*"

sings as a Christian poet of the wonders of the firmament, and yet he is not far removed in

[17] Raphael Pumpelly, *My Reminiscences,* New York, 1920, p. 190.

spirit from the great Aristotle, who has left us this lofty utterance: "Could those men doubt, when they beheld the earth and the sea and the sky with its gathering clouds and its mighty winds, and the glory and majesty of the sun as he floods the heaven with the light of day, and then the starry heaven of night, and the varying brightness of the waxing and waning moon, and the regular movements of all the heavenly bodies and their risings and settings governed by an everlasting and unchanging law, — could they doubt that the Gods really existed and that these mighty works were theirs?" [18]

Even Thomas Hardy is an interpreter of the pagan attitude toward sun-worship when he writes thus: "The sun, on account of the mist, had a curious sentient, personal look, demanding the masculine pronoun for its adequate expression. His present aspect, coupled with the lack of all human forms in the scene, explained the old-time heliolatries in a moment. The luminary was a golden-haired, beaming-faced, mild-eyed, god-like creature, gazing down in the vigor and intentness of youth

[18] A passage from Aristotle's *De Philosophia,* as given by Cicero, *De Natura Deorum,* II, 95. So J. B. Mayor, *Ancient Philosophy,* Cambridge, England, 1895, p. 142.

upon an earth that was brimming with interest to him."[19] It is Thomas Hardy, too, who makes his hero, Jude Frawley, kneel down on the edge of the plateau, turn his face to the rising moon, and repeat Horace's familiar prayer to Diana, the moon-goddess:

P*hoebe, silvarumque potens Diana.*[20]

In the space at our command, it is impossible to do more than merely suggest how rich, varied, and beautiful were the sentiments of the ancient Greeks as inspired by the many phenomena of nature, especially the constellations of the heavens — by the Pleiades and Hyades, by Orion the hunter, by the Dioscuri or "Heavenly Twins," by the morning and evening stars (Phosphorus and Hesperus), by the dawn (Eos or Aurora and Tithonus), by moon-light (Selene and Endymion), by the winds (Boreas and Zephyrus), by the rainbow (Iris). The sea especially was a source of endless interest to these imaginative people, and their myths of Poseidon and Amphitrite, of Thetis and the Nereids, of Proteus and Glaucus and Triton, of Scylla and the Sirens,

[19] *Tess of the D'Urbervilles,* p. 94.
[20] *Jude the Obscure,* Ch. V.

are all indicative of the wonder aroused by the many aspects and moods of the restless, unharvested deep.

Then the streams and fountains — how near they were to the heart and soul of the people, and how much sentiment is wrapped up in the mere name of Alpheus, or Inachus, or Cephisus; of Dirce, Pirene, Callirrhoë or Arethusa! Speaking of the Ilissus, Socrates says: "The stream which flows beneath the plane tree is deliciously cold to the feet. Judging from the ornaments and images, this must be a spot sacred to Achelous and the Nymphs." [21] Thus the cool stream by the plane tree was surely the home of some divinity, to whom the wayfarer might well pay his humble tribute.

"*Then lived the Dryads in yon forest trees;*
Then o'er yon mountains did the Oread roam;
And from the urns of gentle Naïades
Welled the wave's silver foam" [22]

Woods and hills, meadows and brooks, all were peopled with fair forms divine, and the man who lived close to nature could enjoy exalted companionship. The world was young

[21] Plato, *Phaedrus,* 230 B., Jowett's translation.
[22] Schiller, *The Gods of Greece,* translated by Bulwer Lytton.

in those days, and country life was not a life of work alone, but one of worship, as well as of sport, and dance and music.

The rationalist may well tell us that the springs of Greece were sacred because, in an arid land, water must be carefully protected, but the Greeks were more than practical, and offered loving devotion to the beautiful beings who gave them what Pindar calls that "best of all things," pure water. A book of more than seven hundred pages has been written on the "*Springs and Wells in Greek and Roman Literature.*[23] With many of these, beautiful legends are intimately linked, so that by a simple allusion, and without description beyond a mere epithet, a poet may call up a scene of great charm and beauty. Thus in Euripides Pirene and Dirce are simply *holy*, while the fountains of the Hesperides are *ambrosial*.[24]

One of the nature-gods whom we encounter at every turn in post-Homeric literature is Dionysus (Liber or Bacchus).[25] There has been much speculation about the origin and significance of his cult and even of his name.

[23] James R. Smith, New York and London, 1922.
[24] *Med.*, 69; *Tro.*, 206; *Iph. T.*, 401; *Hipp.*, 748.
[25] Also in *Iliad*, VI. 130 ff., xiv. 325; *Odyssey*, XI. 325, xxiv. 74.

Dionysus, it is now believed, is simply a young Zeus, a Dioscure, whose mother Semele (the name is Thracian or Phrygian for earth) was smitten and consumed by fire, when embraced by the great god of thunder and lightning.[26] Father Zeus rescued the unborn babe and concealed him in his thigh till ready for birth, when he was entrusted to the care of nymphs. Later, as he wandered from land to land, he was attended by a wild troupe of Satyrs, Maenads, and Sileni. He represents the principle of vegetable life, and when in the isle of Naxos Ariadne is awakened by his kiss, it is nature aroused in spring from her long winter sleep. In Attica, as god of the vine, Dionysus was worshipped with enthusiasm, and in the Dionysiac festivals the Attic drama is both born and brought to perfection.

Another son of Zeus, born in Arcadia, is Hermes, the Roman Mercury, who is not merely a herald of the gods, but also the god of herdsmen, and in story closely linked with Apollo. As music and athletics were the shepherd's main amusements, Hermes is patron of both. He is himself fleet of foot and he in-

[26] Paul Kretschmer, *Aus der Anomia,* p. 19. See also J. Rendel Harris, *The Ascent of Olympus,* Manchester, The University Press, 1917, p. 14.

vented the shepherd's lyre and the shepherd's pipe or syrinx.

Pan, the pastoral god, was Hermes' son, and represents the spirit of the woods and mountains of Greece. How near he is to nature can not be told more effectively than in the words of the nineteenth of the *Homeric Hymns:* "Tell me, Muse, concerning the dear son of Hermes, the goat-footed, the two-horned, the lover of the din of revel, who haunts the wooded dells with dancing nymphs that tread the crests of the steep cliffs, calling upon Pan the pastoral god of the long wild hair. Lord is he of every snowy crest and mountain peak and rocky path. Hither and thither he goes through the thick copses, sometimes being drawn to the still waters, and sometimes faring through the lofty crags he climbs the highest peak whence the flocks are seen below; ever he ranges over the high white hills, and ever among the knolls he chases and slays the wild beasts, the god with keen eye, and at evening returns piping from the chase, breathing sweet strains on the reeds. . . . With him then the mountain nymphs, the shrill singers, go wandering with light feet, and sing at the side of the dark water of the well, while the echo moans along the mountain crest, and the god leaps hither and thither, and goes into the midst, with many a step of the dance." [27] It is needless to dwell upon the remarkable feeling for the picturesque revealed in this charming passage, with which we may compare an amazingly beautiful stanza in a choral ode of the *Ion* of Euripides: [28]

> "O *haunts of Pan's abiding*
> O *sentinel rock down-gazing*
> *On the Long-cliff caves dim-glimmering,*
> *Where, with shadowy feet in the dance soft-sliding,*
> *Agraulus' daughters three go pacing*
> *O'er the lawns by Athene's fane dew-shimmering*
> *In moonlight, while upward floats*
> A *weird strain rising and falling,*
> *Wild witchery — wafting notes,*
> O *Pan, from thy pipes that are calling*
> *Out of thy sunless grots!*"

But of all the gods of Greece, not one can claim a greater antiquity than the Earth Mother who in early Cretan art occupies the position which Zeus assumes in the later Olympian circle. This Earth Mother was once

[27] Translated by Andrew Lang.
[28] Euripides, *Ion,* 492 ff. (Translation by Arthur S. Way).

supreme at the Pythian oracle,[29] and Aeschylus has the priestess of Delphi offer her the first prayer:

> "*Before all other gods to Earth I call*
> *In prayer, for first was she in oracles;*" [30]

while Pausanias [31] has preserved for us the ancient formula used by the priestess of Dodona: "The Earth yields fruits, therefore glorify Mother Earth," a simple and early version of the Homeric Hymn to Gaia (or Ge), as well as of Coleridge's well-known *Hymn to the Earth:*

> "*Earth! thou mother of numberless children, the nurse and the mother,*
> *Hail! O Goddess, thrice hail! Blest be thou! and, blessing, I hymn thee!*"

In Greek mythology, however, the functions of the Earth Mother have been distributed somewhat widely, for besides Gaia, the Roman Terra, we have Rhea or Cybele, the Magna Mater of Rome, as well as Demeter, or Ceres, goddess of agriculture, and her daughter Kore (Persephone or Proserpina). But functions

29 Cf. Euripides, *Iphigenia in Tauris,* 1234 ff.
30 *Eumenides,* 1 f.
31 X. 12.10.

and rites originally hers are to be found with other goddesses not commonly associated with the Earth. Thus "to Hera she lent her 'sacred marriage,' to Demeter her mysteries, to Athena her snakes, to Aphrodite her doves, to Artemis all her functions as 'Lady of the Wild Things.'"[32] With any of these the Greek feeling for nature may find beautiful expression and perhaps the most notable example of this is in the splendid ode in the *Medea*,[33] where under the graceful garb of mythology, the Attic poet gives utterance to profound emotions evoked by the beauty of his native land:

"*And the streams of Cephisus the lovely-flowing*
They tell how the Lady of Cyprus drew,
And in Zephyr-wafts of the winds sweet-blowing
Breathed far over the land their dew.
And she sendeth her Loves which, throned in glory
By Wisdom, fashion all virtue's story,
Over her tresses throwing, throwing,
Roses in odorous wreaths aye new."[34]

[32] Harrison, *Mythology*, p. 65. *Cf.* John Buchan, *The Dancing Floor*, p. 34: "'The Greeks had only the one goddess,' he went on, 'though she had many names.'"
[33] *Medea*, 824 ff.
[34] Translation by A. S. Way.

In these charming verses, Euripides sings of Aphrodite as breathing the fragrant breath of her life over the Attic land, while, crowned with garlands of roses, she sends the Loves, her offspring, to wait upon Wisdom and Virtue. Have we not here the same romantic spirit which we find in Horace's delightful picture of spring?

Iam Cytherea choros ducit Venus imminente luna,
Iunctaeque Nymphis Gratiae decentes
Alterno terram quatiunt pede.[35]

With Venus herself as leader, the Nymphs and Graces, like modern elves and fairies, dance hand in hand in the woods,

"*While overhead the moon*
Sits arbitress."

The scene is just as romantic as that depicted in art by Sandro Botticelli in his famous "Spring," for Aphrodite was the goddess of spring, associated with flowers and gardens, with the moist earth, with awakening animal life, as well as with the sea, for it was in spring-time that sailors resumed their shipping after the stormy months of winter. It would be

[35] Horace, *Odes,* I. 4. 5 ff. See Shorey and Laing's note on the passage.

easy to follow up this use of Aphrodite (or Venus) in much later literature, where the goddess still holds sway as at least a symbol of nature's beauty. Thus Rémy Belleau (1528–1577) can speak of April as the month when Aphrodite was born of sea-foam:

Mais moy je donne ma voix
A ce mois
Qui prend le surnom de celle[36]
Qui de l'escumeuse mer
Veit germer
Sa naissance maternelle.

It is this mythological and religious background that we must keep in mind at all times as we read Greek and Roman poetry. Take, for example, the ode of Horace which is perhaps most familiar to us all, "O fons Bandusiae" (III. 13), in which is pictured a lovely fountain, clearer than crystal, whose waters, cool and refreshing in summer's sultriest days, leap with cheery prattle from the base of oak-crowned rocks. "An unapproachable model," says Showerman, "of vividness, elegance, purity and restraint." And yet Horace has introduced an element which to many is inexplicable

[36] Aphrodite — April. The poem is *Avril,* written 1565.

and positively offensive, for he is to offer to the fountain a young kid, whose crimson blood will dye those stainless waters. But how natural it was for the pagan poet to make this sacrifice is illustrated by a passage in Ovid's *Fasti* (III. 294 ff.) where we read that King Numa comes to offer a sheep to the fountain at the foot of the dark Aventine grove, that trickled down from a moss-covered rock, for there would a visitor say, *numen inest,* "surely a divinity dwells here!"[37]

An understanding of the pagan religious spirit will help us to appreciate numerous references to rivers and mountains which otherwise must be somewhat unintelligible. Thus river- and mountain-gods are real beings, which, in their power and might, may be either friendly or hostile to man. When Odysseus, after the wreck of his raft, came in the course of his swimming in the sea "over against the mouth of a fair-flowing river," and felt the running of the stream, he prayed earnestly for aid to the god of the unknown water, at whose knees he avows himself a suppliant.[38]

[37] On "O fons Bandusiae," see A. Y. Campbell, *Horace, A New Interpretation,* pp. 1–3, 70 ff., 211–212, London, 1924; Ruskin, *Aratra Pentelici,* 88.
[38] *Odyssey,* V. 441 ff.

So too, the father of Asteropaeus is the son of wide-flowing Axius,[39] and Orsilochus is descended from the Alpheus,[40] Achilles dedicates his hair to the Spercheus,[41] and Poseidon, as lover of Tyro, assumes the form of the river-god Enipeus.[42] One of the most graphic scenes in the *Iliad* is the story of Achilles' struggle with the river Scamander, who "waxes more wroth in his heart, and seeks in his soul how to ward destruction from the Trojans."[43] Later, when "a dark wave of the heaven-sprung River" was about to overwhelm the son of Peleus, Hera besought the aid of her dear son, Hephaestus, who "made ready fierce-blazing fire," and "against the river turned his gleaming flame." A contest between fire and water is to us intelligible enough, but a contest between a mortal man and a river calls for some imagination, until we recall some such devastation as the raging Mississippi has recently wrought, or some startling picture such as Hogarth has given in "The Wandering Scholar" of a scene in Crete: "The river now filled the whole valley from hill to hill. . . . Gnarled planes and centenarian holm-oaks

[39] *Il.*, XXI. 139.
[40] *Od.*, III. 487.
[41] *Il.*, XXIII. 144.
[42] *Od.*, XI. 235.
[43] *Il.*, XXI. 136 ff.

from the river-gorge, with olives and charubs, telling the fate of the higher gardens and orchards, rode past us in an endless tumult — all horribly tangled with horned carcasses, which were sucked spinning below, to be spewed up again, and swept to the sea. *It was a Homeric combat between flood and flood.*" [44]

In this connection we may recall Horace's description of the destruction wrought in Rome by the overflowing Tiber,[45] in whose love for Ilia, ancestress of the slain Caesar, the poet finds a motive for the sending of this ruinous flood. For a benignant picture of "Father Tiber, to whom the Romans pray," we may turn to the peaceful scene at the opening of the Eighth *Aeneid,* where the god visits the hero in his sleep: "It was night, and over all lands deep sleep held wearied creatures, birds and beasts alike, when Father Aeneas, his heart troubled by woeful war, stretched him on the bank under the sky's chill cope, and let late sleep steal over his limbs. Before him the very god of the place, Tiberinus of the pleasant stream, seemed to raise his aged head amid the poplar leaves; thin lawn draped him

[44] *The Wandering Scholar,* Oxford, 1925, pp. 164 ff.
[45] Horace, *Odes,* I. 2. 3 ff.

in mantle of gray, and shady reeds crowned his hair. Then thus he spoke to him, and with these words took away his cares."[46]

It is in Virgil, too, that we find some striking passages descriptive of mountain-gods. Thus, as we approach the final struggle in the *Aeneid*, the hero, who gains fresh vigor and stature, as well as fury, is "vast as Athos, vast as Eryx or vast as Father Apennine himself, when he roars with his quivering oaks, and joyously lifts heavenward his snowy head."[47] Here, Athos, Eryx and Father Apennine are mountain-gods, each with divine personality, and for Roman readers perhaps in no better way could an idea of the hero's towering majesty have been conveyed than through this comparison with gigantic mountain-deities.

[46] Virgil, *Aeneid,* VIII. 26 ff. [47] *Aeneid,* XII. 701 ff.

III. ART

The true order of ascent is to use the beauties of earth as steps along which he mounts upwards for the sake of that other beauty . . . until at last he arrives at the end of all learning, the Idea of Beauty itself, and knows what the essence of Beauty really is.[1] PLATO

Oftentimes have I heard Michelangelo discoursing and expounding on the theme of love, and have afterwards gathered from those who were present that he spoke precisely as Plato wrote. . . . He loved not only the beauty of human beings, but in general all fair things, as a beautiful horse, a beautiful dog, a beautiful piece of country, a beautiful plant, a beautiful mountain, a beautiful wood, and every site or thing in its kind fair and rare, admiring them with marvellous affection.[2]

Earth and Ocean seem
To sleep in one another's arms, and dream
Of waves, flowers, clouds, woods, rocks, and all that we
Read in their smiles, and call reality.[3] SHELLEY

AS WE have found abundant evidence for a deep appreciation of nature in the mythology and religion of the Greeks, so we may gather not a little more from their expression of the beautiful in the sphere of art.

[1] *Symposium,* 210.

[2] Richard Le Gallienne, *Old Love Stories Retold,* p. 202. The speaker is Condivi, beloved pupil and biographer of Michelangelo.

[3] *Epipsychidion.*

Among the remarkable discoveries made by Sir Arthur Evans and others in Crete, one of the most significant is the evidence of an early art on Greek soil which delighted in representing plant and animal forms. The numerous frescoes found at Cnossos, Phaistos and Hagia Triada, the abundant gem- and seal-designs, the exquisite pottery with naturalistic paintings, such as Mrs. Boyd Hawes exhibits in her beautiful book on Gournia,[4] all testify to a wide-spread love of external nature in the Minoan Age, and all the more remarkable because no adequate parallel can be found in the whole range of later Greek art. Here are lilies and crocuses, bulls and antelopes, fish and fowl, octopuses and other kinds of sea-life — an amazing variety of forms from the world of external nature.

In the later Mycenaean age, though art has become more conventionalized, we find similar designs both in such splendid works as the gold cups from Vaphio in the Peloponnesus (possibly heirlooms from an earlier period), decorated with figures of bulls seen amid rocks, olives and palms, and in the richly enamelled

[4] *Gournia, Vasiliki, and other Prehistoric Sites on the Isthmus of Hieropetra, Crete,* Philadelphia, The American Exploration Society, 1908.

dagger-blades from Mycenae, with vivid representations of lions and gazelles, together with fish and fowl in a stream, and papyrus on the banks.

This kind of naturalism is all the more remarkable, because no satisfactory parallel can be found in later Greek art until we reach the Hellenistic age, and even then the evidence is somewhat meagre. We can, to be sure, cite the decorative, and presumably symbolic, use of vegetable and animal forms on coins, gems, and vase paintings,[5] and we may note the slight hint of landscape given by the pebbles on the shore in the famous marble relief from the "Ludovisi Throne," which is generally believed to represent the birth of Aphrodite.[6]

In the Hellenistic period, however, we get interesting reliefs with landscape backgrounds, such as the famous marble panel in the Lateran Museum, which shows a beautiful nymph giving a drink of water to two infants, a Pan and a Satyr. Pan stands within a stone grotto, beside which rises an oak tree. Sheep and goats press close to its foot, while in its

[5] H. N. Fowler and J. R. Wheeler, *Greek Archaeology,* New York, 1909, pp. 353 ff.

[6] E. A. Gardner, *Six Greek Sculptors,* London, 1910. p. 53.

branches various birds and small animals look down upon the scene. In Vienna another of these reliefs portrays a peasant taking a cow to market, while two other reliefs, showing respectively a sheep and a lioness with young, have a vent for water. All of them, perhaps, were originally used to decorate well-heads.[7]

In the days of Augustan Rome, naturalism in art again comes into its own. However dependent the Romans were upon their Greek teachers in painting and sculpture, they certainly have left us ample evidence of their eagerness to surround themselves with artistic reproductions of outdoor life, whether in marble, stucco, or frescoes. The house of Germanicus on the Palatine is decorated with wall-paintings of flowers, fruits and foliage in graceful festoons. A fresco from the villa of Livia at Prima Porta is a beautiful garden-scene, in which various plants are very distinctly grouped, while numerous altars, memorial slabs, and sarcophagi are adorned with trailing vines, climbing roses, oak chaplets, and ivy sprays, carved in no merely conventional

[7] Fowler and Wheeler, *Greek Archaeology*, p. 282; E. Löwy, *Die griechische Plastik*, Leipzig, 1911, fig. 285–287. cf., also, E. Löwy, *Rendering of Nature in early Greek Art* (Engl. tr.), London, 1907.

fashion, but reproduced from nature. Birds and bees, and other forms of animal life are exquisitely wrought. The decorative sculptures of the famous Ara Pacis of Augustus witness not only to great artistic skill, but to a contemporary enthusiasm for reproducing in marble some of nature's most beautiful shapes, as seen in plant and animal life.

In the rich collection of first century frescoes preserved from Pompeii and Herculaneum we have a goodly number of pictures with landscape features, but the chief impression derived from this recovered art is that the people in these buried towns loved to decorate their homes with dainty paintings of the flowers, shrubs, and fruits that doubtless grew in profusion in their walled-in gardens. Surely we can here detect that inborn feeling for nature which we still speak of as Italian.[8]

It is to the credit of the Romans that they resisted the purely conventional treatment of plant forms that we see, for example, in Greek architecture. To quote Mrs. Strong: " To those who are familiar with the conventional forms of the lotus in Egyptian art or of the

[8] On Roman art, see Strong's *Roman Sculpture from Augustus to Constantine;* Geikie's *The Love of Nature Among the Romans,* Ch. VIII.

PLATE II. A ROMAN MOSAIC

From Africa

acanthus in Greek art, it is almost a surprise that even the political Imperial plants, the symbolic laurel, the oak, and the olive, were never conventionalized, but showered their shapely leaves and fruit over every space artistically available." [9]

Though naturalism is thus seen to be characteristic of only early and late periods in Greek art, as well as of the Roman art which followed, the question still remains whether in other, including its greatest, days — the famous fifth century B.C. — Greek art offers any testimony as to a sympathetic attitude toward nature.

In the first place, it has often been remarked that the Greeks generally built their shrines and temples at picturesque sites. We have only to think of the lofty Acropolis of Athens, of " Sunium's marble steeps," of the wild gorge at Delphi, and of the noble outlook at Girgenti over the Sicilian Sea.

" *The lively Grecian, in a land of hills,*
Rivers and fertile plains, and sounding shores, —
Under a cope of variegated sky,
Could find commodious place for every God." [10]

[9] Strong, *Roman Sculpture,* p. 76, quoted by Geikie.
[10] Wordsworth, *The Excursion,* Book IV.

To be sure, Greece is seldom unpicturesque, and the necessity of a defensive site for settlement — a hill-top or deep defile — may account sufficiently for the location of a community's holy places, but a better reason than these is found in the probability that the more picturesque a spot is, the more likely it is to be the home of some divinity: *numen inest!* Thus we see that the foundation of each temple was due to the spirit of religious reverence, and to this spirit we have already appealed for evidence of a deep-seated and genuine appreciation of the mystery and power of nature. And well has Ruskin put the truth, that Pagan religious thought did not "consist only, or chiefly, in giving personality to the gods. The personality was never doubted; it was visibility, interpretation, and possession that the hearts of men sought.[11]

But the stately temple itself, in which the Pagan houses his god, and so gets *possession* of him, has it anything to do with nature's beautiful forms? The glorious fluted columns may suggest the forest trees which once supported the canopy over the god's image; the triglyphs of the frieze with the *guttae* and the

[11] Ruskin, *Aratra Pentelici,* § 34.

mutules may be traced back to constructions in wood; the summit of the Ionic shaft may still be adorned with a band of vegetable forms; and the Corinthian capital may be embellished with a double row of acanthus leaves, but in every case naturalism has given way to convention.

And yet, as Rhys Carpenter has pointed out,[12] there was an opposite tendency at work, for Greek art "imitates the animate . . . Greek artists showed little fondness for portraying inanimate nature," and they developed "a sort of symbolism in terms of animate objects. . . Dolphins stand for the sea, fresh water fish for rivers, a heron for marsh-land, a swan for a lake. At times this symbolism seems forced, as when a naiad stands for a spring of virgin water, or a man-headed bull for a roaring stream; but that is because we today have dropped out an essential link in the chain, and forgotten how the Greek mind peopled fountain, tree, and hill, and river, with local divinities — an instance of this same process of animating natural phenomena by visualizing them in animal or human form."

[12] *The Esthetic Basis of Greek Art* (of the Fifth and Fourth Centuries B.C.), Bryn Mawr Notes and Monographs, 1921.

Let us recall the glorious heads of divinely human beings which we see on the finest of Greek coins. Surely it is not fanciful to suppose that the lovely head of Arethusa on Syracusan decadrachms (Pl. III) reflects the beauty of the fountain dedicated to this nymph. "She is pellucid," says Lucian, "and bubbles up in perfect purity; the water as bright over her pebbles as if it were a mass of silver."[13]

A good illustration of this principle is to be found in the mode of representing localities in temple sculpture. Thus the corner figures in the eastern pediment of the temple of Zeus at Olympia, represent, according to Pausanias, two rivers of Elis, the Alpheus and the Cladeus. The reclining nymphs of the western pediment must also serve to localize the central scene. But far the best illustration of this use of animate forms for animate and inanimate nature is afforded by the famous Parthenon pediments. These splendid groups include a number of figures, whose identity has been the subject of much discussion. In the western

[13] Lucian, *Dialogues of the Sea Gods,* III. Translation of H. W. and F. G. Fowler, Oxford, Clarendon Press, 1905. And yet the Fowlers impute to Lucian "absolute indifference to the beauties of nature!" See their Introduction, p. xxxii.

PLATE III. ARETHUSA
On a Coin of Syracuse

pediment, which exhibited the contest of Athena and Poseidon for the possession of Attica, the scene of action was naturally indicated by some Athenian landmarks, and therefore the reclining figures in the angles are properly identified as personifications of nature, presumably the rivers Cephisus and Ilissus. The surviving nymph on the right is probably Callirrhoë.

In the eastern pediment the birth of Athena was represented. Here, in the left angle, the sun-god Helios is driving his horses toward the scene, while in the right, the moon-goddess Selene is departing with her steeds. Facing the Sun, a youthful nude giant is seated at ease upon some animal's skin spread over a rock. This splendid figure (Pl. IV), commonly known as "Theseus," is identified by Brunn as "the genius of Mount Olympos, upon whose side the rising Helios is driving his horses, and on whose summit is the seat of the gods, and the scene of the action represented in the pediment."[14] Beyond the "Theseus" are two seated female figures, to whom Iris is bearing news of the central event. They are in-

[14] Charles Waldstein, *Essays on the Art of Pheidias*, Cambridge, England, 1885, p. 144.

terpreted as the Horae, who on Olympus had charge of the gates of heaven (*Iliad,* v. 749 ff.). On the other side, that of Selene, there survive three female figures, which are generally regarded as the most beautiful extant specimens of ancient sculpture. They are commonly spoken of as the "Three Fates," though some would make them daughters of Cecrops, and Brunn regards them as personifications of the clouds. But it has been pointed out that one figure is separated from the others, and therefore the three do not form a group. The detached figure may well be Hestia (the Roman Vesta), representing the human family, and as for the remaining two, one of which reclines in the other's lap, Waldstein has quite convincingly proved that they are personifications of the earth and the sea (Gaia and Thalassa). The birth of Athena is conceived as an event of cosmic importance, of interest to heaven, earth and sea, as well as to the human race.

The horses of Helios and Selene are surely the finest horses ever wrought in sculpture, and in themselves are proof that the Greek artist was a keen observer of animal forms. As to the other figures which we regard as personifications of nature, we may well ask the question

PLATE IV. MOUNT OLYMPUS

From the Eastern Pediment of the Parthenon

whether the artists who wrought them (one hesitates to give all the credit even to Pheidias) have not in their magnificent success expressed their own profound appreciation of nature's beauties, for not only do they seem to have caught that vision of ideal Beauty of which Plato in the *Symposium* speaks so eloquently, but they have succeeded in reproducing some phases of it for succeeding ages to enjoy. Perhaps, then, the Parthenon sculptures furnish the most convincing evidence we can present of the Greek love and enthusiasm for nature.

IV. AGRICULTURE AND OUTDOOR LIFE

Agriculture used to be entirely a question of religion; now it is almost entirely a question of science.[1]

GILBERT MURRAY

But not only by reason of grain fields, of meadows, vineyards and woodland, is country life delightful, but also by reason of gardens and orchards, the pasturing of cattle, the swarms of bees, and the flowers of every variety.[2]

CICERO

The husbandman is of all men the most apt to surrender to the discretion of Heaven and take its blows without thought whether they be deserved. Slave of the soil which he turns, to it he looks for all his being.[3]

DAVID G. HOGARTH

My father's sense of beauty in nature was strangely limited. To him the sea was a wild enemy of man and he had no praise for it. Mountains had no place in his esteem. I recall a remark of his on one occasion when we had climbed together to the summit of the mountain, on whose side I was born. He turned toward the wide expanse of cultivated fields, rich with ripening grain, bordered with green meadows, with herds of cattle quietly feeding in them, and set in the centres, the peaceful farm buildings, the abodes of human beings, and he said, 'A bonnie howe (valley) that.' Then, turning toward the west, with the higher Grampians in the distance, with the

[1] *Four Stages of Greek Religion*, p. 18.
[2] *De Senectute*, XV. 54.
[3] *The Wandering Scholar*, p. 171.

snow lying in their black arms, in mid-summer, he called out, — 'A cauld cruel place yon.'[4] GEORGE A. GORDON

IT IS hardly necessary to dwell upon the close association in early days between agriculture and religion. In primitive times, indeed, man must have realized very vividly how dependent he was for mere existence upon the supernatural powers whom he had to propitiate and win over as allies. His life was not one of freedom. It was lived in the bondage of fear. Wild beasts, floods, earthquakes, plagues — all such dangers threatened him, and only the powers unseen — his gods — could give him safety and protection.

So with early pastoral and farming life. However able man had become to protect himself, yet his flocks and herds also were exposed to peril, and neither he nor they, unaided, could escape from the lion, tiger or wolf; "from lightning and tempest; from plague, pestilence, and famine." Then, too, his crops were absolutely dependent on earth, air, and sky. If the unseen powers were kindly, all went well; if hostile, all went ill. Prayer and sacrifice, therefore, entered largely into the

[4] *My Education and Religion*, p. 21, Boston and New York, 1925.

farmer's daily routine, and *ora* as well as *labora* became a rule of life. "Pray to Zeus of the Earth," says Hesiod,[5] "and to pure Demeter, to make Demeter's holy grain sound and heavy," and Virgil, at the beginning of his beautiful *Georgics,* calls upon "all the gods and goddesses, whose love guards the fields, both those who nurse the young fruits, springing up unseen, and those who on the seedlings send down from heaven plenteous rain."[6]

For light upon Greek agriculture, we naturally turn first to the *Works and Days,* a didactic epic, written as early as the ninth century B.C. by a poet of Boeotian Ascra. It is largely a letter of admonition, addressed to a lazy brother, Perses, for whose improvement Hesiod makes use of myth, fable, and precept. Perses is urged to turn from the easy path of vice, and to take the up-hill path of virtue. "Work then, high-born Perses, that hunger may hate you, and venerable Demeter, richly crowned, may love you and fill your barn with food."[7]

This exhortation to work is supported by

[5] Hesiod, *Works and Days,* 465 f. Evelyn-White's translation in *The Loeb Classical Library* is commonly used.

[6] Virgil, *Georgics,* I. 21 ff.

[7] *Works and Days,* 299 ff.

many wise sayings. " Gods and men are angry with the idle man"; "an evil shame is the needy man's companion"; "base gain is as bad as ruin"; "sacrifice to the gods with clean hands and heart, burn rich meats to them, and propitiate them with libations and incense." So, "if your heart desires wealth, do these things, and work with work upon work." It is this Hesiodic call to work which many centuries later Virgil made the corner-stone of his polished *Georgics,* in which he sings for Roman towns the song of Ascra,[8] and which Merivale has aptly characterized as "the Glorification of Labour."[9]

Hesiod is so severely practical that he does not give us many of those pleasing pictures which we should expect in nature poetry. That he was a close observer, however, is seen from a reference to the speckle-necked nightingale (203), from his expression "gray springtime," where the epithet is explained by the gray husks that in spring still cover the buds,[10] and from his striking comparison of the young leaves at the top of the fig-tree to a crow's

[8] *Georgics,* II. 176.

[9] Merivale, *History of the Roman Empire,* Vol. IV, last chapter.

[10] πολιὸν ἔαρ, 477, 492. *Cf.* Evelyn-White's note.

foot-prints. In early spring, when you first see these, you may know that the sea is passable.[11] Hesiod has that reverence for flowing water,[12] the loss of which in modern England shocked Ruskin,[13] but the ancient writer lived at a time when all rivers were regarded as divine, all being children of Ocean and Tethys.[14] Never should you cross them afoot, " until you have prayed, gazing into the soft flood, and washed your hands in the clear, lovely water." [15]

Hesiod's most familiar descriptions are those of summer and winter. Summer has come " when the artichoke flowers, and the chirping grass-hopper sits in a tree and pours down his shrill song continually from under his wings in the season of wearisome heat. . . . At that time let me have a shady rock and wine of Biblis, a clot of curds and milk of drained goats with the flesh of an heifer fed in the woods, that has never calved, and of firstling kids; then also let me drink bright wine, sitting in the shade, when my heart is satisfied with food, and so, turning my head to face the fresh Zephyr, from the overflowing spring which pours down unfouled thrice pour an

[11] II. 678–681.

[12] II. 737 ff.; 758 f.

[13] *Aratra Pentelici.*

[14] Hesiod, *Theogony,* 337–370.

[15] *Works and Days,* 737–739.

offering of water, but make a fourth libation of wine." [16] A dull life this Boeotian farmer led, though not without some bodily comforts.

Unattractive as the summer is, the winter is to Hesiod a season of utter desolation. "Avoid the month Lenaeon,[17] wretched days, all of them fit to skin an ox, and the frosts which are cruel when Boreas blows over the earth. He blows across horse-breeding Thrace upon the wide sea and stirs it up, while earth and the forest howl. On many a high-leafed oak and thick pine he falls and brings them to the bounteous earth in mountain glens: then all the immense wood roars and the beasts shudder and put their tails between their legs, even those whose hide is covered with fur; for with his bitter blast he blows even through them although they are shaggy-breasted. He goes even through an ox's hide; it does not stop him. Also he blows through the goat's fine hair. But through the fleeces of sheep, because their wool is abundant, the keen wind Boreas pierces not at all; but it makes the old man curved as a wheel. And it does not blow through the tender maiden who stays indoors with her dear mother . . . on a winter's day

[16] 582–596. [17] January-February.

when the Boneless One[18] gnaws his foot in his fireless house and wretched home. . . . Then the horned and unhorned denizens of the wood, with teeth chattering pitifully, flee through the copses and glades, and all, as they seek shelter, have this one care, to gain thick coverts or some hollow rock. Then, like the Three-legged One,[19] whose back is broken and whose head looks down upon the ground, like him, I say, they wander to escape the white snow."[20]

Hesiod farmed on a small scale in foggy Boeotia, and for sunnier pictures of Greek rural life we must turn elsewhere. The typical Homeric farmers may probably be found in Laertes and Eumaeus. The former, once a king, but now retired, has a well-built house, with adjacent farm-buildings and laborers' dwellings. He cultivates figs and olives, pears and vines, and had once given his young son Odysseus, to be his very own, thirteen pear-trees, ten apple-trees, and forty fig trees, promising him fifty rows of vines with corn sown between.[21]

[18] i.e. The octopus or cuttle.

[19] i.e. the old man walking with a staff, as in the riddle of the Sphinx.

[20] *Works and Days,* 504–535.

[21] *Odyssey,* XXIV. 205 ff., 244 ff., 336 ff.

Eumaeus, the swineherd, was himself of princely birth, but having been kidnapped in infancy by Phoenicians, was later sold to Laertes, and then brought up on an intimate footing with the royal family of Ithaca. As he drew near to manhood he was given a responsible position on Odysseus' large estate, and may be regarded not merely as a swineherd, but also as a kind of bailiff or overseer. He had built himself a house and swinery and, had it not been for his master's absence and the suitors' presence, he would have received a good home with three acres of land and a wife. As it is, he is able to give the stranger a bountiful supper of pork, bread and wine.[22]

Another charming picture is furnished by the famous garden of Alcinous in the Phaeacian land,[23] and delightful glimpses of rural life may be seen in many of the Homeric similes and in the pictures adorning the shield of Achilles.[24] There we can see the rich ploughland, the ripe cornfield with the reapers and binders at work, the master looking on in contentment, and the servants preparing a meal for all, and the vineyard heavy with purple grapes. As these are

[22] *Odyssey*, XIV. 5 ff., 55 ff.
[23] *Odyssey*, VII. 112 ff.
[24] *Iliad*, XVIII. 478 ff.

gathered into woven baskets, young men and maidens dance to the music made by a boy, who plays the harp and sings a sweet strain. Sheep, too, dot the meadow, and the cows are lowing by a running brook.

A whiff of country air comes from some simple folk-songs which have survived. Here is a flower-song,[25] which children sang in alternating groups:

"*Where are my roses? where are my violets? where are my beautiful parsley-leaves?*"
"*Here are your roses; here are your violets; here are your beautiful parsley-leaves.*"

And in Rhodes, on a day in early spring, the children would go round the town seeking presents from door to door, and singing the advent of the swallow: [26]

"*She is here, she is here, the swallow!*
Fair seasons bringing, fair years to follow!
Her belly is white
Her back black as night!

. . . .

Whatever you give, give largess free!
Up! open, open to the swallow's call!
No grave old men, but merry children we!"

[25] *Lyra Graeca*, III. p. 536 (Edmonds).
[26] *Ibid.* p. 526. (J. A. Symonds). *Cf.* Athenaeus, VIII, 360 B.

These swallow-songs are still sung in Greece, and as for flowers, their beauty is sung all through Greek literature, especially in lyric poetry and the *Anthology*.

As to the Greek drama, we should bear in mind that this whole field — tragedy as well as comedy — has the distinctly rustic background of the festivals of Dionysus. "The god embodied the spirit of country life, and tragedy came into existence under the most rural of rural conditions." [27] Of the plays of Aristophanes, two deal very directly with country life, the *Acharnians* and the *Peace*. In the former, Dicaeopolis, a country farmer, being tired of the long war, makes his own peace with the enemy, and in the latter, Trygaeus would have his fellow-husbandmen deliver Peace herself from the pit into which the divine being had fallen. Both plays set forth the pleasures of country life in the piping days of peace, when one may enjoy

> "*Figs and olives, wine and myrtles,*
> *Luscious fruits preserved and dried,*
> *Banks of fragrant violets, blowing*
> *By the crystal fountain's side.*" [28]

[27] Martinengo-Cesaresco, *The Outdoor Life in Greek and Roman Poets*, p. 26.

[28] Aristophanes, *Peace*, 575 ff. Translation by B. B. Rogers.

Xenophon, best known for his historical works, wrote also some rural treatises, the *Oeconomicus*, *Hippike*, and *Cynegeticus*. In these he has left us a very vivid and pleasing picture of himself as a gentleman-farmer, who loved his dogs and horses, and can speak with authority of ploughings and fallowings, of manuring and draining land, and all such details as would be of interest to the intelligent owner of a handsome country estate. He was an out-of-doors man, who, after his thrilling experiences with the Ten Thousand in Asia, was glad to settle down in the prime of life on the broad acres in the Peloponnesus which a grateful Sparta had given him. Here he found that leisure and retirement which appeal so strongly to the English gentry and more and more to cultivated Americans.

The next great writer who is primarily concerned with the open country is the pastoral poet Theocritus (3d century B.C.), whose shepherds and goatherds are invested with an immortal charm and whose joy in the external world makes him for us supreme among the nature-poets of Greece.

All so-called "pastoral poetry" in the world's literature centres in Theocritus, and all of it, of whatsoever merit, implies a fundamental admiration and love for nature, which is more true, more genuine, the nearer it comes to Theocritus. But pastoral poetry, as a type, is not in high repute, because at certain periods it has seemed too far removed from the realities of life. Thus the Arcadia romances of the sixteenth century, whether in Italy, Spain, or England, clothe the sentiment in a garb of elaborate fiction, and in the court pastorals of the seventeenth and eighteenth centuries, the "last remnants of simplicity were abandoned," the utmost extreme of artificiality being reached by French pastoralism, in comparison with which all antecedent forms seem to breathe pure naturalism. And yet, running through all these artificial disguises, there is a certain vein of fancy which is true, because it is the upwelling of a love for nature.

In Theocritus this love of nature is universally conceded to be genuine, but we do not always realize how accentuated it is by standing out so clearly against the drab background of the artificial Alexandrine age. The Idylls are an expression of a revolt from this unnatural life, and of a yearning for a return to nature. Far be it from me to introduce a discordant note into the chorus of admiration for Theocritus, but when I realize that it is the very unnaturalness of the age that moved Theocritus to express his own love of nature so clearly and so beautifully, I ask myself whether we are fair to the other great minstrels of Greece, when we laud him as the nature-poet *par excellence,* and by inference depreciate those who, living very close to nature, entertain a sentiment for her which, though fully as sincere, is expressed in forms less familiar to us, but more truly Greek.

In this chapter, however, we are following the lower slopes of Parnassus, and we are to think of Theocritus not so much as nature's hierophant, but merely as one portraying the more obvious features of Sicilian country-life with its shepherds, herdsmen, reapers, fishermen, and other sons of toil. In one of his epic idylls he shows us agriculture on a large scale, for in the " Hercules, the Lion Slayer," he describes the farm or ranch of King Augeas, which we may suppose resembled some lordly Sicilian estate in the days of Hieron. Augeas is the owner of fleecy flocks, that feed on many pastures along the river-banks, with separate pens for each flock; also of countless cattle, grazing on the luscious meadows around the marsh, but stalled at night near a river, where one may see luxuriant plane-trees and a grove of wild-olives. In long rows of huts are housed the country-folk, who sow the grain in season, and plough the vast wheat-fields three or even four times a year. Vineyards, orchards and fountains complete the picture.[29]

A contemporary and friend of Theocritus aspired to be the Hesiod of Alexandria. The *Phaenomena* of Aratus, dealing with astronomy and the signs of the weather, may be regarded as a sort of farmers' calendar, which proved of service to Virgil in the composition of the *Georgics*. The philosopher Theophrastus, a disciple of Aristotle, continued his master's studies in the life of nature and wrote two books on botany, which have survived.

In Italy, agriculture played a dominant part from the earliest days of the Roman state, and farming was always in high repute as an occupation. The traditions and history of Rome are closely linked with country life, and the surviving works of the Roman *Scriptores Rei Rusticae,* including Cato, Varro, Columella,

[29] Theocritus, *Idyll,* XXV. 7–33.

Palladius, and Vegetius, are among the most valuable and remarkable documents of antiquity. Besides these practical writers on the farmer's art, we have numerous glimpses of country life in such prose-writers as Cicero and Pliny the Elder, but the best pictures are found in all the great poets, especially Lucretius, Catullus, Virgil, Horace, Tibullus and Ovid. The amount of available material for studying the Roman attitude toward nature is therefore quite ample, and most of it must necessarily be omitted from our survey. Indeed we shall here content ourselves with citing only two of these writers, Cicero for prose, and Virgil for poetry.

In the *Cato Maior De Senectute* Cicero makes the aged Cato his ideal example of an active, useful, and happy old age. Cato was a farmer who had risen from the plough to the highest honors in the state, and it is fitting therefore that, in meeting the charge that old age is devoid of pleasures, he should not only prove that old age is capable of the greatest intellectual enjoyment, but should also exhibit an enthusiasm for agriculture, which had been his main pursuit in life, and upon which he had written so fully in his own *De Re Rustica.*

"In the pleasures of the farmer," he tells us, "I take an incredible delight, for they are hampered by no old age, and, to my mind, they approach most nearly to the philosopher's ideal life. Farmers keep an account with Earth herself, and she never fails to recognize their rights, and never returns their deposits without some interest, occasionally small, but generally large. Yet it is not only in the returns, but in the natural powers of the soil that I find delight" — and this idea Cato expands at considerable length. He takes special pride in the culture of vines and in the various modes of plant propagation. "What," he exclaims, "can be pleasanter to enjoy? what fairer to look upon?" "Indeed," he concludes, "to my mind no life can be happier, not only because of service rendered, for agriculture is helpful to all mankind, but also because of the pleasure enjoyed. . . There can be nothing more truly beneficial, nothing more beautiful in appearance than a farm well cultivated." [30]

And no less enthusiastic is Virgil. The word *laetus* in the very first sentence of the *Georgics* gives the key-note to the whole poem, through which runs a strain of joyful earnestness. "O

[30] Cicero, *Cato Maior de Senectute*, XV. 51–XVI. 57.

ye most radiant lights of the firmament . . . and ye, O Fauns, the rustics' ever-present gods (come trip it, Fauns, and Dryad maids withal!), 'tis of your bounties I sing."[31] And in this spirit he calls men to the labor of the fields: "In the dawning spring, when icy streams trickle from snowy mountains, and the crumbling clod breaks at the Zephyr's touch, even then would I have my bull groan over the deep-driven plough, and the share glisten when rubbed by the furrow. That field only answers the covetous farmer's prayer, which twice has felt the sun and twice the frost; from it boundless harvests burst the granaries."[32] Then, after the admonition to study the special conditions of the soil, for one region differs from another in its natural products, Virgil continues: "Here corn, there grapes spring more luxuriantly; elsewhere young trees shoot up, and grasses unbidden. See you not, how Tmolus sends us saffron fragrance, India her ivory, the soft Sabaeans their frankincense; but the naked Chalybes give us iron, Pontus the strong-smelling beaver's oil, and Epirus the mares that win Olympian victories?"[33]

[31] Virgil, *Georgics,* I. 5 ff.
[32] *Ibid.* 43 ff. [33] *Ibid.* 54 ff.

Work is a law of nature, which man and beast should follow; "come then, and where the earth's soil is rich, let your stout oxen upturn it straightway, in the year's first months. . . . Yea, and much service does he do the land who with mattock breaks up the sluggish clods, and drags over it wicker hurdles; nor is it for naught that golden Ceres views him from high Olympus. . . For moist summers and sunny winters pray, ye farmers! With winter's dust most gladsome is the corn, gladsome is the field: under no tillage does Mysia so glory, and then even Gargarus marvels at his own harvests." [34]

Listen to the poetry of irrigation: "Need I tell of him who flings the seed, then, hoe in hand, closes with the soil, and lays low the hillocks of barren sand? next brings to his crops the rills of the stream he guides, and when the scorched land swelters, the green blades dying, lo! from the brow of the hillside channel decoys the water? This, as it falls, makes a hoarse murmur amid the smooth stones, and with its gushing streams slakes the thirsty fields." [35] No modern poet, not even Angela Morgan in her spirited "Work,"

[34] *Ibid.* 63 ff. [35] *Ibid.* 104 ff.

has glorified labor more beautifully than Virgil.

In the Second Book, with fresh enthusiasm, the poet becomes himself a fellow worker with Bacchus in the vintage. "Come hither, O Lenaean sire, strip off thy buskins and with me plunge thy naked legs in the new must. . . Up! therefore, ye husbandmen, learn the culture proper to each after its kind; your wild fruits tame by tillage, and let not your soil lie idle. What joy to plant all Ismarus with the vine, and clothe great Taburnus with the olive!" [36] We call the *Georgics* didactic, but never was teaching imparted with more burning zeal, for Virgil is full of the "glory of the divine country" [37] and the *Georgics,* besides being replete with practical wisdom, thrill from first to last with the poet's love for his theme:

> O *fortunatos nimium, sua si bona norint,*
> A*gricolas!* [38]

In view of the large part played by agriculture in the life of the ancients, it would be natural for the poets to look upon land and

[36] Virgil, *Georgics,* II. 7–38.
[37] *divini gloria ruris,* Virgil, *Georgics,* I. 168.
[38] Virgil, *Georgics,* II. 458 f. "O happy husbandmen! too happy, should they come to know their blessings!"

sea largely from the point of view of their utility. Thus Homer frequently calls the earth *ζείδωρος*, 'fruit-bearing,' while he applies to the sea an epithet, *ἀτρύγετος*, which is commonly rendered as 'barren,' or 'unharvested,' as if derived from *τρύγη*, 'ripe fruit.' But to-day scholars are inclined to regard the word as meaning 'unresting.' Be that as it may, we find in Euripides [39] an undisputed reference to the sea's "unharvested plains," *ἀκάρπιστα πεδία*.

As to mountains, it is perhaps due to the same reason — the tendency to judge land in terms of fertility and productiveness — that in ancient poetry we find comparatively few descriptions implying an appreciation of the beauty of mountain-scenery. Professor Hardie, indeed, cites the *Critias* of Plato as containing the only passage in Greek literature which distinctly implies that mountains were considered capable of possessing beauty at all. Here, the mountains surrounding the plain of Atlantis are remarkable "for their number and size and beauty, in which they exceeded all that are now to be seen anywhere"; yet the words following seem to tell us in what that beauty consisted, for the mountains had

[39] Euripides, *Phoenissae*, 210.

"many wealthy inhabited villages, and rivers, and lakes, and meadows supplying food enough for every animal, wild or tame, and wood of various sorts, abundant for every kind of work." [40]

Archilochus certainly speaks in depreciative terms of the mountain heights of Thasos, which "like a donkey's back, stands crowned with wild wood. 'Tis a place by no means fair or lovely or pleasant, as is the land by the streams of Siris." [41] Hardie himself, however, admits that the many epithets applied to mountains by Greek poets imply much appreciation of their beauty, and we shall see that there is considerably more evidence to the same effect, though much of it has been overlooked. At any rate, nowhere in Greek and Roman literature do we find such an attitude toward mountains as is revealed in the striking passage from Dr. Gordon's autobiography which appears at the head of this chapter.

[40] Plato, *Critias,* 118B, Jowett's translation.

[41] See "Tyrtaeus, Archilochus and their Successors" in Warner's *Library of the World's Best Literature,* vol. xxvi, p. 15168. The description of Thasos "is as appropriate now as when Archilochus wrote, the gaunt but picturesque line of its dorsal ridge standing prominently out from its wooded heights" (Tozer, *Geography of Greece,* p. 44).

V. HOMERIC POETRY

As one that for a weary space has lain
  Lulled by the song of Circe and her wine
  In gardens near the pale of Proserpine,
Where that Aegean isle forgets the main,
And only the low lutes of love complain,
  And only shadows of wan lovers pine,
  As such an one were glad to know the brine
Salt on his lips, and the large air again,
So gladly, from the songs of modern speech
  Men turn, and see the stars, and feel the free
    Shrill wind beyond the close of heavy flowers
    And through the music of the languid hours,
They hear like ocean on a western beach
  The surge and thunder of the Odyssey.

ANDREW LANG

He scarce had finish'd when such murmur fill'd
The assembly as when hollow rocks retain
The sound of blustering winds, which all night long
Had roused the sea, now with hoarse cadence lull
Sea-faring men o'erwatched, whose bark by chance,
Or pinnace, anchors in a craggy bay
After the tempest.[1] MILTON

As in the country, on a morn in June,
When the dew glistens on the pearlèd ears,
A shiver runs through the deep corn for joy —
So when they heard what Peran-Wisa said
A thrill through all the Tartar squadrons ran.[2]

MATTHEW ARNOLD

[1] *Paradise Lost,* II. "Though no servile imitator of Homer in detail, our English poet is here strikingly Homeric." W. C. Green, *The Similes of Homer's Iliad,* p. 211, London and New York, 1877.

[2] *Sohrab and Rustum,* cf. *Iliad,* XXIII, 597 ff.

If we observe his *descriptions, images,* and *similes,* we shall find the invention still predominant. To what else can we ascribe that vast comprehension of images of every sort, where we see each circumstance of art and individual of nature summoned together, by the extent and fecundity of his imagination; to which all things, in their various views, presented themselves in an instant, and had their impressions taken off to perfection, at a heat? Nay, he not only gives us the full prospects of things, but several unexpected peculiarities and sideviews, unobserved by any painter but Homer.[3] POPE

The developed similes of Homer, without counting those more slightly stated, exceed two hundred and thirty, of which only about forty are in the Odyssey.[4] GLADSTONE

Es liebte dich früh die heilige Natur!
Weihte dich und säugte dich an ihrer Brust![5]
STOLBERG

HOMER, says the German poet Stolberg, owes his greatness to Nature herself, and Schiller speaks of Homer as the simple, naïve poet who is always in unconscious harmony with Nature. Matthew Arnold, too, regards Homer as the very antithesis of the modern sentimental poet, and emphasizes the plainness and directness, not merely of his style, but also of his ideas. Plainness and directness, indeed, are the most char-

[3] Preface to his translation of the *Iliad.*
[4] *Homer,* p. 150.
[5] *Homer,* cited by Max Batt, *The Treatment of Nature in German Literature,* p. 58.

acteristic features of Homer's attitude toward nature, and may be seen best in the similes which are so conspicuous a feature of the *Iliad* and the *Odyssey*.

Take for the first example the famous comparison of the Trojan fires on the plain to the stars of heaven. Could anything be more simple and yet more beautiful?

> "*As when in heaven the stars about the moon*
> *Look beautiful, when all the winds are laid,*
> *And every height comes out, and jutting peak*
> *And valley, and the immeasurable heavens*
> *Break open to their highest, and all the stars*
> *Shine, and the Shepherd gladdens in his heart:*
> *So many a fire between the ships and stream*
> *Of Xanthus blazed before the towers of Troy.*"[6]

Equally simple and picturesque is the comparison of two heroes to a ridge that rises from a plain:

> "*Behind them still the Ajaces checked the foe,*
> *As checks the water some long spur of land,*
> *Shaggy with wood, that juts athwart the plain;*
> *Which stems the impetuous flow of mighty floods*
> *And plainwards swiftly turns the stream of all,*

[6] *Iliad*, VIII. 555 ff., translation by Tennyson. This is quoted, with numerous other examples, by Palgrave, *Landscape in Poetry*.

Driven from their beds — nor may they break its dam
Though strong the current's race: so did these twain
Hold back the Trojans' onset from behind." [7]

As the two armies, " bristling with shields and helms and spears," sit facing each other on the plain, eagerly awaiting Hector's challenge to single combat, it is as when " there is spread over the face of the deep the ripple of the West Wind, that is newly risen, and the deep groweth black beneath it." [8]

Equally direct is the famous comparison of the generations of men to the leaves of the forest: " Even as are the generations of leaves, such are those also of men. As for the leaves, the wind scattereth some upon the earth, but the forest, as it bourgeons, putteth forth others when the season of spring is come; even so of men one generation springeth up and another passeth away." [9]

Of similes that are both simple and brief, let us note how a smitten warrior " bows his head

[7] *Iliad,* XVII. 746 ff., translation by W. C. Green, " The Similes of Homer's Iliad."

[8] *Iliad,* VII. 63 ff. This and most of the translations from Homer are by A. T. Murray, in *The Loeb Classical Library,* 1919 and 1924.

[9] *Iliad,* VI. 147 ff. Translation by A. T. Murray.

to one side like a poppy that in a garden is laden with its fruit and the rains of spring";[10] and how the words of Odysseus, when on an embassy to Troy, were "like snowflakes on a winter's day."[11]

Similarly in the *Odyssey,* the hero's raft is driven hither and thither along the sea, even "as the North Wind in the harvest tide sweeps the thistle-down along the plain, and close the tufts cling each to other."[12] Presently the beams of the raft are torn apart, "as when a great tempestuous wind tosseth a heap of parched husks, and scatters them this way and that."[13]

When Penelope wept floods of tears, as she heard the tales told by her unrecognized husband, it was "even as the snow melts in the high places of the hills, the snow that the South-east wind has thawed, when the West has scattered it abroad, and as it wastes the river streams run full."[14] And for a brief and pointed simile, could anything be simpler and clearer than the comparison of Odysseus' shin-

10 *Iliad,* VIII. 306 ff. Translation by A. T. Murray.
11 *Iliad,* III. 222.
12 *Odyssey,* V. 328 ff. Butcher and Lang's translation.
13 *Odyssey,* V. 368 ff. (Butcher and Lang.)
14 *Odyssey,* XIX. 205 ff. (Butcher and Lang.)

ing doublet to "the skin of a dried onion, so smooth it was, and glistening as the sun"?[15]

A study of Homer's numerous similes, as Pope and Jebb have observed, reveals "a spontaneous glow of poetical energy,"[16] and, we may add, a remarkable familiarity with aspects of nature. The poet is not content with confining himself to points of comparison, but frequently adds seemingly irrelevant details, which, while having no direct bearing on the similitude proper, bring the known aspect into greater relief, and so enable us to picture the unknown circumstance more clearly. The poet, in other words, has more familiarity with the natural feature cited than is required by his comparison. He "not only gives us the full prospects of things, but several unexpected peculiarities and side-views, unobserved by any painter but Homer."[17] For an illustration of this principle Jebb cites the passage in the Eighteenth *Iliad,* where the flame flashing from the cloud above Achilles' head is compared to the beacon fire sent up by a beleaguered city, and where over and above the comparison proper, some details of the siege are added.

[15] *Odyssey,* XIX. 232 ff. (Butcher and Lang.)
[16] Jebb's *Homer,* p. 27.
[17] Pope, Preface to his translation of the *Iliad.*

So too in the simile given above from the Eighth *Iliad,* the shepherd's joy is an added touch, which is not essential to a comparison between the fires on the plain and the stars of heaven.

The most conspicuous natural features in Homer's similes and descriptions are the mountains and the sea. Mountains are "many-fountained"[18] (and Tennyson takes his "many-fountained Ida" from the Eighth *Iliad*), but they are lonely places,[19] for a mountain is a mother of wild beasts,[20] such as boars,[21] and lions, that "upon the mountain-tops are reared by their dam in the thickets of a deep wood,"[22] as well as of dangerous serpents,[23] and huge eagles, such as the wide-winged black eagle which Zeus sent from Ida as a sign to Priam.[24]

Odysseus dwells "in clear-seen Ithaca, wherein is a mountain Neriton, with trembling forest leaves, standing manifest to view."[25]

[18] cf. *Iliad,* VIII. 47, XIV. 157, XX. 59.

[19] For οἰοπόλος of mountains, see *Odyssey,* XI. 574; *Iliad,* XXIV. 614 and XIX. 377.

[20] μητέρα θηρῶν of Ida, *Iliad,* VIII. 47.

[21] *Iliad,* XII. 146.

[22] *Iliad,* V. 554.

[23] *Iliad,* XXII. 93.

[24] *Iliad,* XXIV. 315 ff.

[25] *Odyssey,* IX. 21 ff.

Olympus, " seat of the gods," is to be pictured in contrast to the mountains known to men, for while the earthly Olympus is capt with snow,[26] here there

> " *falls not hail, or rain, or any snow,*
> *nor ever wind blows loudly.*" [27]

The gleam of bronze as the troops march forth is like a fire which makes a boundless forest blaze on mountain-peaks,[28] and the dust beneath the feet of tramping men is like a mist which the South Wind sheds over the mountain-heights,[29] while the Danaans, when holding their own against the Trojans, are " like mists that in still weather the son of Cronos setteth on the mountain-tops moveless, what time the might of the North Wind sleepeth and of the other furious winds that blow with shrill blasts and scatter this way and that the shadowy clouds." [30] But when both armies march into action, it is " as when winter torrents, flowing

26 ἀγάννιφος, *Iliad,* I. 420. The comparison, in *Iliad,* XIII. 754, of Hector to a snowy mountain can be explained only by the theory that he is supposed to resemble a mountain god. See pp. 30–33 above.

27 Tennyson's description of the island valley of Avilion is like Homer's picture of Olympus, *Odyssey,* VI. 43. *Cf.* however *Odyssey,* IV. 566 (the Elysian plain).

28 *Iliad,* II. 455 ff.

29 *Iliad,* III. 10.

30 *Iliad,* V. 522 ff.

down the mountains from their great springs to a place where two valleys meet, join their mighty floods in a deep gorge, and far off amid the mountains the shepherd heareth the thunder thereof." [31]

Two warriors, standing firm before the advancing foe, are like "oaks of lofty crest among the mountains, that ever abide the wind and rain day by day, firm fixed with roots great and long." [32] When two armies join in fierce conflict, it is as when "the East Wind and the South strive with one another in shaking a deep wood in the glades of a mountain — a wood of beech and ash and smooth-barked cornel, and these dash one against the other their long boughs with a wondrous din, and there is a crashing of broken branches;" [33] and when the Danaans at last thrust the Trojans back from the ships, it was "as when from the high crest of a great mountain Zeus, that gathereth the lightnings, moveth a dense cloud away, and forth to view appear all mountain peaks, and high headlands, and glades, and from heaven breaketh open the infinite air," [34] — a superb picture of mountain scenery, such

[31] *Iliad,* IV. 450 ff.
[32] *Iliad,* XII. 132 ff.
[33] *Iliad,* XVI. 765 ff.
[34] *Iliad,* XVI. 297 ff.

as one often sees in beautiful Switzerland after rain.

But the sea figures even more largely than mountains in Homer's pictures from nature. The poet is never far from her, and can look upon her in all her moods and aspects.

Not seldom, indeed, mountain and sea are brought together, as when Helen regrets that on the day of her birth a storm had not carried her off "to some mountain or to the wave of the loud-resounding sea"; [35] or when the missiles flung by two warring armies are compared to flakes of snow, falling thick until they cover "the peaks of the lofty mountains and the high headlands, and the grassy plains, and the rich tillage of men; aye, and over the harbors and shores of the gray sea is the snow strewn, albeit the wave as it beateth against it keepeth it off, but all things beside are wrapped therein, when the storm of Zeus driveth it on"; [36] or again, when the clamor of battle is likened to the bellowing of the sea upon the shore, or to "the roar of blazing fire in the glades of a mountain, when it leapeth to burn the forest, nor doth the wind

[35] *Iliad*, VI. 345 ff.

[36] *Iliad*, XII. 278 ff.

shriek so loud amid the high crests of the oaks." [37]

The noise of mustering troops is like "a wave of the loud-resounding sea thundering on the long beach," [38] and as soldiers march into battle, it is "as when on a sounding beach the swell of the sea beats, wave after wave, before the driving of the West Wind; out on the deep at the first is it gathered in a crest, but thereafter is broken upon the land and thundereth aloud, and round about the headlands it swelleth and reareth its head, and speweth forth the salt brine"; [39] and again when the Trojans advance shouting, it is "as when at the mouth of some heaven-fed river the mighty wave roareth against the stream, and the headlands of the shore echo on either hand, as the salt-sea belloweth without." [40]

"The surge and thunder," mentioned by Andrew Lang in his beautiful sonnet,[41] is really more in evidence in the *Iliad* than in the *Odyssey,* and one more good illustration occurs in the Thirteenth Book, where, led by Hector, the Trojans advance "like the blast of direful winds that rusheth upon the earth beneath the

[37] *Iliad,* XIV. 394 ff.

[38] *Iliad,* II. 209 f.

[39] *Iliad,* IV. 422 ff.

[40] *Iliad,* XVII. 263 ff.

[41] Quoted on p. 67.

thunder of father Zeus, and with wondrous din mingleth with the sea, and in its track are many surging waves of the loud-resounding sea, high-arched and white with foam, some in the van and after them others." [42]

The sudden squalls and violent hurricanes, so familiar to travelers in the Aegean, furnish numerous similes. Thus Hector's arrival on the battle-field is "like a blustering tempest, that leapeth down and lasheth to fury the violet-hued deep"; [43] and he assails the foe "even as when the West Wind driveth the clouds of the white South Wind, smiting them with a violent squall, and many a swollen wave rolleth onward, and on high the spray is scattered beneath the blast of the wandering wind." [44]

Quieter aspects of the sea are often presented to us, and one of Tennyson's favorite hexameters [45]

ἐξ ἀκαλαρρείταο βαθυρρόου Ὠκεανοῖο,

pictures the "softly-gliding, deep-flowing Oceanus" from which rises the morning sun.[46]

[42] *Iliad,* XIII. 795 ff.
[43] *Iliad,* XI. 297 f.
[44] *Iliad,* XI. 305 ff.
[45] *Iliad,* VII. 422; *Odyssey,* XIX. 434.
[46] See Wilfred P. Mustard, "Tennyson and Homer," in *The American Journal of Philology,* XXI. 143–153 (1900).

It was no blind poet who wrote the passage from which we learn how far the horses of Hera could spring at a bound, even " as far as a man seeth with his eyes into the haze of distance as he sitteth on a place of outlook and gazeth over the wine-dark deep." [47] When the ranks of the Achaeans and Trojans are seated on the plain, it is " even as there is spread over the face of the deep the ripple of the West Wind, that is newly risen, and the deep groweth black beneath it "; [48] but when the Achaeans are in deep distress over the loss of their noblest men, it is " even as two winds stir up the teeming deep, the North Wind and the West Wind, that blow from Thrace, coming suddenly, and forthwith the dark wave reareth itself in crests and casteth much tangle out along the sea." [49] The quiet heaving of the sea, ominous of a coming storm, is suggested by Nestor's anxious

[47] *Iliad,* V. 770 ff.

[48] *Iliad,* VII. 63 ff. In view of Tennyson's familiarity with Homer, it is not at all improbable that the familiar lines in " The Lady of Shalott,"

> " Little breezes dusk and shiver
> Thro' the wave that runs forever,"

were suggested by this simile. Cf. the μέλαινα φρίξ of *Iliad,* XXI. 126, and *Odyssey,* IV. 402, and see Mustard, *op. cit.,* p. 153.

[49] *Iliad,* IX. 4 ff.

mind,[50] but when Apollo lightly casts down the Achaeans' wall, the poet is reminded of a child playing in the sand beside the peaceful water and merrily scattering the structures he has taken such pains to build.[51]

But like the lonely mountains the sea can be soulless and pitiless, as Patroclus well knew, for he is sure that the inexorable Achilles must be the offspring, not of Thetis and Peleus, but of the gray sea and the beetling cliffs.[52]

Extended descriptions of places in Homer are almost confined to the *Odyssey,* which thus illustrates one side of its truly romantic character. Of some of these it may be said that they are given from a purely agricultural point of view. Thus the isle of Syria is "a good land, rich in herds, rich in flocks, full of wine, abounding in wheat."[53] The Cyclopes live in a land where everything "springs up for them without sowing or ploughing, wheat, and barley, and vines,"[54] and Ithaca is a rugged isle, not fit for driving horses, yet not utterly poor, though it be but narrow. Therein grows corn beyond measure, and the wine-grape as well,

50 *Iliad,* XIV. 16 ff.
51 *Iliad,* XV. 361 ff.
52 *Iliad,* XVI. 33 ff.
53 *Odyssey,* XV. 403 ff.
54 *Odyssey,* IX. 109 f.

and the rain never fails it, nor the rich dew. It is a good land for pasturing goats and kine; there are trees of every sort and in it also pools for watering that fail not the year through.[55] The Phaeacian king, Alcinous, has "a great orchard of four acres, and a hedge runs about it on either side. Therein grow trees, tall and luxuriant, pears and pomegranates and apple-trees with their bright fruit, and sweet figs, and luxuriant olives. Of these the fruit perishes not nor fails in winter or in summer, but lasts throughout the year; and ever does the West Wind, as it blows, quicken to life some fruits, and ripen others; pear upon pear waxes ripe, apple upon apple, cluster upon cluster, and fig upon fig." There is also a vineyard which is carefully described, and "trim garden foods of every sort," and two springs. All these were "the glorious gifts of the gods in the palace of Alcinous."[56]

These descriptions do not rest on a high level of sentimental appreciation, but this quality may easily be recognized in the famous account of Calypso's isle, the sight of which delighted the heart of even the divine messenger of Zeus:

[55] *Odyssey,* XIII. 242 ff. [56] *Odyssey,* VII. 112 ff.

"*Around the cave there grew a lusty wood,*
Alder and poplar and sweet-smelling cypress,

Wherein far-winging birds were wont to nest —
Falcons and owls and chattering-tongued sea-crows
That have their business on the sea; and there
About the cavern trailed a garden vine
Robust and cluster-laden, and four fountains
All in a row were running with bright water,
Hard each by each, but facing different ways.
Around, soft meadows bloomed with violets
And parsley. E'en a god who chanced to come
Might gaze and marvel and delight his heart." [57]

Seldom has any poet expressed his love of trees and vines and flowers and running water in more charming fashion.

In the last quoted passage, the poet reminds us of the birds that nest in the woods, and a catalogue of Homer's birds would include, besides the

"*Falcons and owls and chattering-tongued sea-crows,*"

the domestic fowl, doves, geese and swans, swallows, starlings, thrushes, daws, nightingales, bats, cranes, herons, hawks, eagles, and vultures.

[57] *Odyssey,* V. 63 ff. Morris' translation.

The range of domestic animals is wide, including dogs, horses, sheep, cattle, asses, and mules. Other creatures are bees and wasps, gadflies, locusts, serpents, dolphins and the fish-tribe. Wild animals are equally numerous, such as hares and deer besides leopards and jackals, wolves, boars and especially the lion. The lion is mentioned chiefly in similes, at least twice in the *Odyssey,* but some thirty times in the *Iliad,* where he appears in many striking comparisons. Thus Menelaus foretells that Odysseus will descend upon the cowardly suitors in his home, even as a lion comes upon new-born fawns, which a mother-hind has laid to sleep in his lair before ranging the mountain slopes in quest of pasture.[58] And Ajax, defending the body of the fallen Patroclus, "stands as a lion over his whelps, exulting in his strength and drawing down all his brows to cover his eyes.[59] Surely a naturalist must take great delight in the fauna as well as the flora of Homer, who lived close to nature, and knew her in so many aspects. In the vividness of his pictures of animal life, Dante comes nearest to Homer, for strikingly Homeric are many of his similes. Take, for example, the

[58] *Odyssey,* XVII. 124 ff. [59] *Iliad,* XVII. 132 ff.

passage where a fiery serpent darts on his victim "swift as a lizard, who, in the heat of the dogstar, flashes like lightning from wall to wall across the road." [60] Compare too the way in which sinners rise up from the pitchy lake "like dolphins that with the upraised arch of their backs give mariners a token of approaching storm, and as swiftly do they disappear." [61] These examples are taken from W. C. Green's "The Similes of Homer's *Iliad*," which gives many interesting parallels from Virgil, Dante, Spenser, Milton, and Matthew Arnold, as well as occasional ones from Lucan, Shakespeare, Dryden, Tasso, and Scott.

The *Homeric Hymns*, so called because antiquity ascribed them, as well as the epics, to Homer, really belong to various periods running from the seventh century B.C. to the Christian era. These poems contain many echoes of the epics, and certain aspects of the Homeric attitude toward nature naturally reappear, but in their romantic narratives there are some distinctive passages that deserve to be cited. In the *Hymn to Delian Apollo* the god is thus addressed: "Everywhere, O Phoebus, the whole range of song is fallen to you, both over the

[60] Dante, *Inferno*, XXV. 79. [61] *Inferno*, XXII. 19.

mainland that rears heifers and over the isles. All mountain-peaks and high headlands of lofty hills and rivers flowing seawards and havens of the sea are your delight. Shall I sing how at the first Leto bore you to be the joy of men, as she rested against Mount Cynthus in that rocky isle, in sea-girt Delos — while on either hand a dark wave rolled on landwards driven by shrill winds — whence arising you rule over all mortal men?"[62] The objects of the sun-god's delight — mountain peaks, rivers and sea-beaches, are surely the poet's delight as well.

> "*And the blue noon is over us,*
> *And the multitudinous*
> *Billows murmur at our feet*
> *Where the earth and ocean meet,*
> *And all things seem only one*
> *In the universal sun*"[63]

Another passage is in the *Hymn to Aphrodite,* and may be quoted to illustrate with what religious reverence the Greeks looked upon their mountains and the great trees growing on their heights. The child Aeneas is to be

[62] *Homeric Hymns,* III. 20 ff. Translation by Evelyn-White.

[63] Shelley, *The Invitation.*

brought up by the "deep-breasted mountain nymphs who inhabit this great and holy mountain. They rank neither with mortals nor with immortals: long indeed do they live, eating heavenly food and treading the lovely dance among the immortals . . . but at their birth pines or high-topped oaks spring up with them upon the fruitful earth, beautiful, flourishing trees, towering high upon the lofty mountains (and men call them holy places of the immortals, and never mortal lops them with the axe); but when the fate of death is near at hand, first those lovely trees wither where they stand, and the bark shrivels away about them, and the twigs fall down, and at last the life of the Nymph and of the tree leave the light of the sun together." [64]

The *Hymn to Pan* presents a very attractive picture of the shepherd god, who "has every snowy crest and the mountain peaks and rocky heights for his domain; hither and thither he goes through the close thickets, now lured by soft streams, and now he presses on amongst towering crags and climbs to the highest peak that overlooks the flocks. . . Only at eve-

[64] *Homeric Hymns,* V. 257 ff. Evelyn-White's translation.

ning, as he returns from the chase, he sounds his note, playing sweet and low on his pipes of reed: not even she could excel him in melody — that bird who in flower-laden spring pouring forth her lament utters honey-voiced song amid the leaves . . . while Echo wails about the mountain-top, and the god on this side or on that of the choirs, or at times sidling into the midst, plies it nimbly with his feet. On his back he wears a spotted lynx-pelt, and he delights in high-pitched songs in a soft meadow where crocuses and sweet-smelling hyacinths bloom at random in the grass." [65] The poet, who wrote thus, had surely heard the call of the wild, and had felt something of the spirit of him who wrote:

" *Hist! there's a stir in the brush*
Was it a face through the leaves?
Back of the laurels a skurry and rush
Hillward, then silence except for the thrush
That throws one song from the dark of the bush
And is gone." [66]

And finally in the *Hymn to Demeter* there occurs that remarkable passage in which the poet describes the beautiful flower which drew

[65] *Hymn to Pan,* XIX. 6 ff. Evelyn-White's translation.
[66] Richard Hovey, *The Faun.*

Persephone on to her fate, and she was carried off to become the pride of the "Ruler of Many and Host of Many" in the world below. "Apart from Demeter, lady of the golden sword and glorious fruits, she was playing with the deep-bosomed daughters of Oceanus and gathering flowers over a soft meadow, roses and crocuses and beautiful violets, irises also and hyacinths and the narcissus, which Earth made to grow at the will of Zeus and to please the Host of Many, to be a snare for the bloom-like girl — a marvellous, radiant flower. It was a thing of awe whether for deathless gods or mortal men to see: from its root grew a hundred blooms and it smelled most sweetly, so that all wide heaven above and the whole earth and the sea's salt swell laughed for joy."[67] Here heaven, earth and sea, all laugh for joy at the sight of a flower in bloom!

> "*The daffodils were fair to see,*
> *They nodded lightly on the lea,*
> *Persephone — Persephone!*"[68]

[67] *Hymn to Demeter,* II. 4 ff. Evelyn-White's translation.
[68] *Persephone,* by Jean Ingelow.

VI. LYRIC POETRY

Awake, Aeolian lyre, awake,
And give to rapture all thy trembling strings.
From Helicon's harmonious springs
A thousand rills their mazy progress take:
The laughing flowers that round them blow
Drink life and fragrance as they flow.

. . . .

Woods, that wave o'er Delphi's steep,
Isles, that crown th' Aegean deep,
Fields, that cool Ilissus laves,
Or where Maeander's amber waves
In lingering lab'rinths creep,

. . . .

Where each old poetic mountain
Inspiration breath'd around;
Ev'ry shade and hallowed fountain
Murmur'd deep a solemn sound.

THOMAS GRAY

The isles of Greece, the isles of Greece!
Where burning Sappho loved and sung,
Where grew the arts of war and peace,
Where Delos rose, and Phoebus sprung!
Eternal summer gilds them yet,
But all, except their sun, is set. BYRON

A brighter Hellas rears its mountains
From waves serener far;
A new Peneus rolls his fountains
Against the morning star.
Where fairer Tempes bloom, there sleep
Young Cyclads on a sunnier deep. SHELLEY

O wanderer from a Grecian shore,
Still, after many years, in distant lands,
Still nourishing in thy bewildered brain
That wild, unquenched, deep-sunken, old-world pain —
Say, will it never heal?
And can this fragrant lawn
With its cool trees, and night,
And the sweet, tranquil Thames,
And moonshine, and the dew,
To thy racked heart and brain
Afford no balm?

MATTHEW ARNOLD

Thalatta! Thalatta!
Sei mir gegrüsst, du ewiges Meer!
Sei mir gegrüsst zehntausendmal
Aus jauchzendem Herzen
Wie einst dich begrüssten
Zehntausend Griechenherzen,
Unglückbekämpfende, heimatverlangende,
Weltberühmte Griechenherzen.

HEINRICH HEINE

Arrête! Écoute-moi, voyageur. Si tes pas
Te portent vers Cypsèle et les rives de l'Hèbee,
Cherche le vieil Hyllos et dis-lui qu'il célèbre
Un long deuil pour le fils qu'il ne reverra pas.

JOSÉ-MARIA DE HEREDIA

If any place, if any tongue, can express what I feel, and contain what I worship, it is Greece and Greek.[1]

MAURICE HEWLETT

[1] *The Letters of Maurice Hewlett,* edited by Lawrence Binyon (Methuen).

IT IS in lyric poetry that we commonly expect to find most of our literary evidence as to a nation's appreciation of the beauties of nature.

For several reasons, however, this is not the case with the Greek literature which we may enjoy to-day. In the first place, Greek lyric poetry was essentially song poetry, in which music was an essential element, and as the music has not survived, the poetry associated with it has largely disappeared also, and of the great body of Greek lyric verse which once existed only scraps and fragments have been preserved. In the second place, the only great lyric writers, whose work has come down to us in any completeness, namely Pindar and Bacchylides, wrote choral odes for the public celebration of victories in the national games, and these odes, noble and magnificent as they are, are almost epic in scope, rather than lyric in our sense of the term, and are comparatively free from that personal and individual sentiment which commonly pervades lyric poetry. A third reason lies in the fact that Greek lyrics, after running their course as an independent type of literature, became largely absorbed in the drama, so that many of the finest lyrics in the language must be handled, not as independent songs, but as important elements in tragedy and comedy.

Glancing for a moment at the elegiac and iambic poets of Greece, we may note that, while they furnish little material for our purpose, there is one passage in the sententious Theognis which would startle us with the boldness and beauty of its spiritual feeling, had we not met a similar tone in the *Homeric Hymns*.[2] The poet, addressing Phoebus Apollo, son of Leto, tells how, when his mother goddess bore him, "fairest of immortals, by the encircling lake, all the wide expanse of Delos was filled with ambrosial fragrance, the mighty earth burst into laughter, and the deep gulf of the hoary sea rejoiced."[3] In the response which Nature here makes to the advent of godhead we seem to have evidence of a religious feeling that is not unlike his who once told how "the morning stars sang together, and all the sons of God shouted for joy."[4]

[2] See p. 88.
[3] Theognis, ll. 7–10, in Bergk's *Poetae Lyrici Graeci*, II. p. 118.
[4] *The Book of Job*, XXXVIII. 7.

> "*Time was when field and watery cove*
> *With modulated echoes rang,*
> *While choirs of fervent Angels sang*
> *Their vespers in the grove.*"[5]

Of the nine lyric poets recognized in the Alexandrian canon, the first was Alcman, "whose poems were not made the less sweet because he used the tongue of Sparta."[6] He "knew the tunes of all the birds," and longed to be himself a sea bird and flit with the halcyons "over the wave's bloom, a sea-blue bird of the spring,"[7] the original of Tennyson's

"*sea-blue bird of March*"[8]

Alcman has immortalized his beautiful singers Agido and Hagesichora, for the light of Agido is "bright as the very sun's, which she invokes to shine upon" the maiden singers, and Hagesichora's tresses have the sheen of purest gold.[9] Amid the ambrosial night the two are fairer than the heavenly Doves (i.e. the Pleiades), nay they are as bright as Sirius him-

[5] Wordsworth, "Composed Upon an Evening of Extraordinary Splendor and Beauty."

[6] Pausanias, III. 15.1, referring to an inscription at Sparta. *Lyra Graeca,* I. p. 49 (J. M. Edmonds), in *The Loeb Classical Library.*

[7] Alcman, 67 and 26 (Bergk).

[8] *In Memoriam,* XC. 4; cf. *Memoir,* II. 4.

[9] Alcman, I. 40 ff.; 51 ff.

self, and as for their song, Hagesichora sings like the swan beside the streams of Xanthus.[10]

Alcman glories in the peace of nature, for he sings of the calm sea that "falls dumb upon the shore among the tangle"[11] and of "the wood-beflowered mount of Rhipe, that is the breast of murky night,"[12] while nowhere in Greek literature is there a more simple and impressive picture of midnight calm than in the well-known lines: "Asleep lie mountain-top and mountain-gully, shoulder also and ravine; the creeping things that come from the dark earth, the beasts whose lying is upon the hillsides, the generation of the bees, the monsters in the depths of the purple brine, all lie asleep, and with them the tribes of the winging birds."[13] Professor Wright cites the obvious parallel of Goethe's *Ueber Allen Gipfeln ist Ruh,* and notes that "Alcman omitted the personal application that secures a poetic climax for the German lyric.[14] As for English parallels we naturally think at once of Wordsworth's

[10] Alcman, I. 60, 100 f.

[11] Alcman, 13, in *Lyra Graeca* I (Edmonds).

[12] Alcman, 64 (Edmonds).

[13] *Ibid.* 36 (Edmonds).

[14] Wilmer Cave Wright, *A Short History of Greek Literature,* New York, 1907, p. 107. See, too, H. W. Smyth, *Greek Melic Poets,* London, 1900, pp. 198 f.

"*The silence that is in the starry sky,*
The sleep that is among the lonely hills."[15]

Alcman lived in the middle of the seventh century B.C., and it was about the end of the same century that Alcaeus, the gay cavalier-poet of Mitylene, sang of

dura navis,
Dura fugae mala, dura belli[16]

Only scanty scraps of his famous Aeolic verses remain, but along with the stirring, vigorous, and splendid imagery for which he was renowned, we have evidence that he had an observant eye and a fine feeling for nature.

Thus in his hymn to Apollo, when the young god passed from the Hyperboreans to Delphi, it was the heart of midsummer, when "the nightingale, the swallow and the cicada were singing to mankind the tale of thy fortune, while Castalia flowed with silvery streams, and great Cephisus uplifted his gleaming waves, knowing well that a God was coming to his

[15] *Song at the Feast of Brougham Castle,* II. 163 f. In his *Books and Characters,* pp. 16 ff., Lytton Strachey comes to the defence of Racine's "flat and feeble set of expressions" for a silent night in "Mais tout dort, et l'armée, et les vents et Neptune."

[16] Horace, *Odes,* II. 13. 27–28.

home."[17] Elsewhere, the poet addresses the Sun, "who hast come past river-banks or the gleaming sea, where the splashing wave beats on the foaming shore."[18] He notes "the beginning of flowery Spring,"[19] and "the stormless breath of light winds."[20] He loves the Hebrus, "fairest of all rivers,"[21] and knows the ways of birds, which "cower at the sudden sight of the swift eagle,"[22] while "between earth and snowy sky,"[23] he sees "wild geese, of motley neck and widespread wing, that have come from the ocean and the ends of the earth."[24]

Of all the Greek lyric poets, the one most sensitive to the beauty of nature is undoubtedly the peerless Sappho. This famous Lesbian poetess, who was a contemporary of Alcaeus, has been so fully and ably treated in a separate volume in this series,[25] that it is hardly necessary for me to do more than remind my

17 Alcaeus, 1.
18 *Ibid.* 17.
19 *Ibid.* 166.
20 *Ibid.* 165.
21 *Ibid.* 93.
22 *Ibid.* 21.
23 *Ibid.* 36.
24 *Ibid.* 141.
25 *Sappho and Her Influence,* by David M. Robinson, 1924, in the *Our Debt to Greece and Rome* Series.

readers of the exquisite perfection of Sappho's verse, which owes so much of its charm to her innate love of the beautiful world in which she lived. "All the luxuries and elegancies of life which that climate and the rich valleys of Lesbos could afford . . .; exquisite gardens, where the rose and hyacinth spread perfume; river-beds ablaze with the oleander and wild pomegranate; olive-groves and fountains where the cyclamen and violet flowered with feathery maiden-hair, pinetree-shadowed groves, . . a tideless sea; fruits such as only the southern sun and sea-wind can mature; marble cliffs, starred with jonquil and anemone in spring, aromatic with myrtle and lentisk and samphire and wild rosemary through all the months; nightingales that sang in May; temples dim with dusky gold and bright with ivory; statues and frescoes of heroic forms. In such scenes as these the Lesbian poets lived, and thought of love. When we read their poems, we seem to have the perfumes, colors, sounds, and lights of that luxurious land distilled in verse."

This eloquent passage in Symonds' *Studies of the Greek Poets*[26] furnishes a suitable

[26] Cited by Robinson, p. 25.

setting for the lovely imagery of the Sapphic poems and the abundant references to trees and fruits and flowers — violets, lilies, hyacinths, anthrysc, melilot, anise, and, above all, roses; to birds — doves, halcyons, the "heavenly" swallow, the "clear-voiced" nightingale; to the bright stars and the "rosy-fingered" moon, and to "breezes rustling amid apple-branches by cool waters, where quivering leaves are drowsy with slumber." [27]

The beauty that fills Sappho's world has fascinated the great singers of both ancient and modern times. Catullus and Horace were under the spell of "the poetess." Swinburne's lyric fervor was exalted by her, and in our own day Sara Teasdale has paid a beautiful tribute to her power in a blank-verse poem of two hundred and twenty-five lines, which goes by the Lesbian's own name, while to Hilda Doolittle, known as "H.D." [28] and the most brilliant of the *imagists,* Sappho is undoubtedly the chief literary inspiration.

Among the other lyric poets of Greece the seventh century Stesichorus of Sicilian Himera,

[27] Sappho, 5 in Edmonds' *Lyra Graeca.*

[28] I have dealt with "H.D." in *The Classics and Our Twentieth Century Poets,* pp. 29–36, Stanford University Press, 1927.

and the sixth century Ibycus of Italian Rhegium are interesting figures. The former wrote love-idylls which are the beginning of Greek romantic poetry, and his lost pastoral on Daphnis, not to speak of surviving references to Cydonian apples, myrtle leaves, rose-garlands and violet-wreaths, as well as to the swallow twittering in spring-time, shows his spiritual kinship to the great Sicilian of later days, Theocritus. As for Ibycus, we can detect in his fragments an almost romantic sentiment for external nature, evidenced by his love of fruits and flowers, running brooks and starry nights.

At the beginning of the fifth century flourished the great Simonides of Ceos, so famous for his elegies and choral dirges. It is he who recalls that "saying of the man of Chios,[29] 'The life of man is even as the life of leaves,'" and who reproves Cleobulus of Lindus for supposing that the great tomb of Midas can be as lasting as the ever-running rivers, the flowers of spring, the flame of sun and golden moon, and the eddying of the ocean-waves. These, we may suppose, are the aspects of nature which the poet loves most. He sings

[29] Homer. See p. 70.

too of the birds of "sweet-scented" spring, the "blue swallow, its loud-voiced harbinger," and the "green-necked, much warbling nightingales," of windless halcyon-days, and of the "breeze that ruffles the sea."[30] As to the sea, indeed, there are few more moving passages in literature than the simple lines in which Danaë, afloat in the ark with her sleeping babe, prays that the sea too may sleep, together with her own misery.[31]

Bacchylides, "the nightingale," as he describes himself, "of Ceos,"[32] whose poems were fortunately rescued from the sands of Egypt near the end of the nineteenth century, was a nephew of Simonides. He loves the "fair isle" where he was born, "land of rocky heights," "the nurse of vines," whose cities were "steeped in sunshine."[33]

Bacchylides is fond of the picturesque, and all his odes are full of life and light and color. Automedes outshines his rivals in the pentathlon "even as the brilliant moon of the mid-month night surpasses the stars in radi-

[30] The fragments of Stesichorus, Ibycus, and Simonides referred to, are in Edmonds' *Lyra Graeca,* Vol. II.
[31] Simonides, 13, 15 f.
[32] Bacchylides, 3.98. (*Lyra Graeca,* Vol. III, p. 143.)
[33] 5.10; 1.11; 6.5; 1.29.

ance." [34] The poet uses many single epithets that are expressive of great beauty, and by this and other means he imparts to his narratives a brightness and clarity fundamentally due to his vivid realization of nature's charms. His days are "radiant," his nights "dark-bosomed" and "holy," his sea is "sun-lit" and his river-banks "rose-clad." [35] So too the Muses are "violet-crowned," the Graces "violet-eyed," and the Nereids "violet-tressed." The Morning is "golden-armed," when she looks upon the "tawny-haired," "storm-swift" courser Pherenicus, victorious by the "wide-eddying" Alpheus.[36] Io is the "rosy-fingered" daughter of the river-god Inachus, and Aegina, the island-goddess, herself "gentle-hearted," is one of the twelve daughters of the "purple-eddied" Asopus, "lord of sounding waters." [37]

These daughters of Asopus have each their own distinctive features, for one is "dark-haired," another "fair-robed," and a third "wreath-entwined," while the attributes of the

[34] 8.27 ff.

[35] 18.27, 28. For ἁγνός of night, cf. *heilige Nacht*. Also Fr. 232; Fr. 16, 10. Also 15.34; 5.5; 18.39.

[36] 5.3; 18.5; 16.37; 5.37–40.

[37] 18.18; 12.78; 8.39; 65.

rest are lost.[38] All, presumably, are personifications of places, including Thebes, Nemea and Aegina. Aegina's glory, indeed, is a theme of song and dance, when "a maid of proud bearing, with her glorious neighbors and comrades, moves over thy holy ground, lightly as a joyous fawn on the flowery hills, while, crowned with brilliant blossoms and reeds, they hymn thy power, O mistress of an all-welcoming land." [39] An island-poet, who can thus beautifully enter into the feelings of other islanders, is paving the way for the most striking personification of an island-home which Greek literature can show — that of Cos in the famous Seventeenth Idyll of Theocritus.

And Bacchylides also knew the sea that encompasses those "isles of Greece," for did not his Theseus behold the glory of the Nereids themselves, when he went down to the abode of his father Poseidon? "There with awe he beheld blest Nereus' famous daughters, for a splendor as of fire shone from their radiant forms; fillets inwoven with gold encircled their hair; and they delighted their hearts by danc-

[38] 8.54 ff. The passage is fragmentary, but the full list is given by Diodorus, 4.72. See Jebb's note on 8.49 f.

[39] 12.83 ff. (Mainly Jebb. Also Edmonds, p. 189.)

ing with lissom feet." [40] Yet, with all this delight in ocean's beauty, the poet knew something of its terrors as well, as when "amid the dark bloom of the deep the North-Wind afflicts men's hearts with the surge when it meets them as Night riseth, but with the light-giving Dawn ceaseth, aye and smooths the sea, and they set their sail to fill in the favoring breath of the South-Wind till they reach the unhoped-for haven.[41]

The spirit of Bacchylides is akin to that of Euripides, and in Rome he was much admired by Horace, Tibullus, and, later, by the Emperor Julian. His well-known lines on the blessings of Peace, when "the webs of red-brown spiders are on the iron-bound handles of shields," [42] have left their impress on Theocritus, Nonnos, Ben Jonson, and Lowell,

> "H*ang up my idle armor on the wall*
> *Let it be the spider's banquet-hall,*" [43]

but as only a few fragments of the poems have been known to the modern world until our

[40] 16.101 ff. (Jebb).
[41] 12.124 ff. (Edmonds p. 191).
[42] *Fr.* 3.6 f. (Jebb).
[43] Lowell's *Launfal,* cited by H. W. Smyth, *Greek Melic Poets,* p. 447.

own day, the greater influence of Bacchylides on the world's literature is yet to come.

Bacchylides, however, will never enjoy the same fame that has been won by his elder contemporary Pindar, greatest of all lyric poets of Greece, if not of the whole world. Pindar has left us forty-four triumphal odes, divided according to the four great national contests of Greece, Olympian, Pythian, Isthmian, and Nemean, but only fragments testify to the greater productivity and versatility of a poet, three-fourths of whose work is lost, but who was master in every branch of the lyric art.

This poet-priest of aristocratic lineage, who was known throughout the length and breadth of the Greek world, is distinguished by the stately structure of his verse, by his extraordinary metrical power, by what Sir Philip Sidney called his "gorgeous eloquence," by his vividness of imagery, and his "intoxicating" style, to use the phrase of Matthew Arnold, which combined "opulence and elevation with swiftness and strength."[44] With such a genius and such a reputation, no wonder that in his destruction of Thebes,

[44] Gildersleeve's article on "Pindar" in Charles Dudley Warner's *A Library of the World's Best Literature.*

"*The great Emathian conqueror bade spare*
The house of Pindarus, when temple and tower
Went to the ground." [45]

In his attitude toward external nature, Pindar shows himself to be singularly objective. Nature's beauties are bathed in the atmosphere of brilliance and splendor that illuminates all the flight of "the Theban eagle,"

"*Sailing with supreme dominion*
Thro' the azure deep of air."

In the Islands of the Blest, around which the ocean-breezes blow, golden are the flowers and radiant the trees,[46] and in Elysium, "amid meadows red with roses, the park before the city is shaded by the incense-tree, and laden with fruits of gold."[47] On earth, too, lovely Rhodes is "the bride of the Sun"[48] and when "the Lord of the golden hair" speaks from his oracle to him[49] who is to found a colony there, the worshipper is told to sail to "a pasture sea-ringed, where once the great king of the gods rained on a city a snow-shower of gold."[50] To be sure, "man is a mere dream

[45] Milton, *Sonnet* III.
[46] *Ol.*, II. 71 ff.
[47] *Fr.*, 129.
[48] *Ol.*, VII. 14.
[49] Tlepolemus.
[50] *Ol.*, VII. 32 ff.

of a shadow; but, when a gleam of sunshine cometh as a gift of heaven, a radiant light resteth on men, aye and a life of sweetness."[51] Here surely is Wordsworth's "celestial light," making shine the face of him who wins a Pythian victory, and Pindar's is "the Painter's hand," to

> *"add the gleam,*
> *The light that never was, on sea or land,"*

for all his Odes are resplendent with glory, and Pindar "drains dry the Greek vocabulary of words for light and bright, shine and shimmer, glitter and glister, ray and radiance, flame and flare and flash, gleam and glow, burn and blaze."[52] With good reason does Mrs. Browning speak of "our Pindar's shining goals."[53]

But Pindar comes down to earth from time to time. He knows the "black-clouded plains" of Libya,[54] the "wind-echoing glens of Pelion,"[55] the "vine-clad Mysian plain,"[56] the

[51] *Pyth.*, VIII. 95 ff. Sir John Sandys' *Pindar* in *The Loeb Classical Library*, 1919, and Gildersleeve's edition of *The Olympian and Pythian Odes.*
[52] Gildersleeve's edition, p. xxxvi.
[53] *Wine of Cyprus.*
[54] *Pyth.*, IV. 52.
[55] *Pyth.*, IX. 5.
[56] *Isth.* VIII. 49.

"cliff-girt level of the hoary sea,"[57] the "steepy cliffs of Helorus' banks,"[58] the "sun-bathed hill of Cronus,"[59] "tree-clad,"[60] once "sprinkled with much snow,"[61] the "deep-lying Nemea,"[62] the "lofty-reigning Parnassus,"[63] the "boundless brake" with a wealth of "golden and deep-purple rays of pansies"[64] in the "prime of red-flowered spring,"[65] and the "far-stretching" spaces of Epirus, where cattle-pasturing headlands slope gently down from Dodona to the Ionian sea.[66] It is Pindar who describes Athens as "the shining, the violet-crowned, the sung in story; the bulwark of Hellas, famous Athens, city divine!"[67] The beautiful epithet "violet-crowned" in this fragment of a dithyramb is explained by Gildersleeve as referring to "the amethystine hues of the garland of mountains that encompass Athens." This very plausible explanation is rejected by Professor Sandys, because the Athenian purple glow, seen only at sunset, is peculiar to Hymettus alone, *purpureos colles florentis Hymetti.*[68] But is it not a case of

[57] *Isth.*, IV. 56.
[58] *Nem.*, IX. 40.
[59] *Ol.*, I. 111.
[60] *Nem.*, XI. 25.
[61] *Ol.*, X. 51.
[62] *Nem.*, III. 18.
[63] *Nem.*, II. 19.
[64] *Ol.*, VI. 54.
[65] *Pyth.*, IV. 64.
[66] *Nem.*, IV. 51 ff.
[67] *Fr.*, 46.
[68] Ovid, *Ars. Am.* III. 687.

metonomy, a part for the whole or *vice versa?* In any case, " Athens lies in an amphitheatre of beautiful mountains." [69]

The most detailed description in Pindar occurs in his account of an eruption of " snow-clad " Aetna, that " forehead of a fruitful land," " a column reaching to heaven and nursing keen frost the live-long year." [70] It is Aetna,

> " *Whose founts of fire*
> *Gush from her caves, most pure, untamable:*
> *And all day well*
> *The rivers, and the gleaming smoke-wreath's spire;*
> *And in the gloom of night —*
> *A lurid purple-light —*
> *The flame upheaves vast rocks and with a roar*
> *Whirls them far out upon the ocean-floor.*
> *It is yon monster makes outpour these dire*
> *Volcanic torrents: wondrous to behold,*
> *A monster e'en to hear by others told*
> *How pinioned*
> *'Neath dark-cleaved heights of Aetna and the plain*
> *He writhes in pain."* [71]

[69] *A Glimpse of Greece,* by Edward Hutton, London, 1928, p. 17.
[70] *Pyth.,* I. 19, 20, 30.
[71] *Pyth.,* I. 21 ff., translated by A. G. Newcomer in Warner's *A Library of the World's Best Literature* (under " Pindar ").

Numerous fragments of the minor poets of Greece often remind us of the rich abundance of lyric song which the ancients once enjoyed, and some of these surviving verses may serve to illustrate our theme. Thus Ion of Chios, who wrote dithyrambs as well as tragedies in the great fifth century, was called in heaven the 'Star of Morn,' because one of his songs began thus: "Let us wait for the Star of Morn that haunts the sky, the white-winged forerunner of the Sun."[72] A similar jest is made at the expense of Praxilla, also of the fifth century, who in one of her poems had Adonis descend to Hades, where, being asked what was the most beautiful thing he had left behind in the world above, he replied: "The fairest thing I leave is the sunlight, and fairest after that the shining stars and the face of the moon, aye and ripe cucumbers and apples and pears." This remark, Zenobius tells us, gave rise to a saying, "sillier than Praxilla's Adonis," for "only a simpleton would put cucumbers and the like on a par with the sun and the moon."[73] But perhaps to Adonis or

[72] *Lyra Graeca,* III. pp. 226–7 (Edmonds).
[73] *Lyra Graeca,* III. pp. 72–75 (Edmonds).

Praxilla, as to Wordsworth, "every common sight"

"did seem
Apparelled in celestial light,
The glory and the freshness of a dream." [74]

[74] *Ode on Intimations of Immortality.*

VII. THE GREEK DRAMA

Consider the seasons, the joy of the spring, the splendor of the summer, the sunset colors of the autumn, the delicate and graceful bareness of winter trees, the beauty of snow, the beauty of light upon water, what the old Greeks called the unnumbered smiling of the sea.[1]

VISCOUNT GREY OF FALLODON

Listen! you hear the grating roar
Of pebbles which the waves draw back and fling,
At their return, up the high strand
Begin, and cease, and then again begin,
With tremulous cadence slow, and bring
The eternal note of sadness in.[2] MATTHEW ARNOLD

He flung back his head and quoted some sonorous Greek. "What's that?" I asked. "Euripides," he replied. "It has been well translated," and he quoted:

For her breath is on all that hath life, and she floats in the air
Bee-like, death-like, a wonder.[3] JOHN BUCHAN

Aristophanes, "the half divine humorist in whose incomparable genius the highest qualities of Rabelais were fused and harmonized with the supremest gifts of Shelley."

SWINBURNE

Romanticism will exist in human nature as long as human nature itself exists. The point is (in imaginative literature) to adopt that form of romanticism which is the mood of the age.[4] THOMAS HARDY

[1] *Fallodon Papers,* p. 76. *Cf.* p. 134 below.
[2] *Dover Beach.*
[3] *The Dancing Floor,* p. 35.
[4] *The Early Life of Thomas Hardy,* p. 189.

GREEK TRAGEDY is a mixture of the lyric and dramatic elements, wholly lyric in its origin and more and more dramatic as it develops, yet never losing the lyrical feature. In such a play as the lost *Phoenissae* of Phrynichus the chorus was the chief actor, and Phrynichus was famous for his songs, one of which indeed is the original of the familiar lines from Thomas Gray:

> " O'*er her warm cheek and rising bosom move*
> T*he bloom of young Desire, and purple light of Love.*" [5]

In Aeschylus, the *Suppliants* is mainly a lyrical play, and even the *Agamemnon,* though one of the greatest of dramas, has the two longest choral passages in extant Greek tragedy. In Sophocles, the lyrical element is carefully subordinated to the dialogue, the two elements form a beautiful harmony, and Sophoclean tragedies are the most truly representative of Attic dramatic art. With Euripides we see the beginning of disintegration, for the chorus is no longer a vital element in the play, though it remains an element of great beauty, and

[5] *The Progress of Poesy,* cited by Wright, *Greek Literature,* p. 190.

indeed seldom, if ever, in the extant Euripidean plays can the choral songs be shown to be mere interludes, or wholly inappropriate to the tragic theme or situation.

It follows that the Greek dramatists' love of nature's beauties will most commonly find expression in the choral passages, though we must not confine our attention to these, for in works of art so charged with emotion many an utterance on the lips of an actor will be essentially lyrical. It is largely, however, this sharp contrast between the two elements in Greek tragedy that accounts for the comparative lack of color and sentiment in the dialogue when examined side by side with that of the Shakespearian or modern romantic drama, where speeches are often pitched in a more lyrical tone. Such passages as the following,

"*Methought I heard a voice cry, 'Sleep no more,'*"

or Hamlet's

"*To be or not to be,*"

or Wolsey's

"*Farewell, a long farewell to all my greatness!*"

would in a Greek play find their place in the lyrics of the chorus rather than in the speeches of the actors.

Apart from this fundamental feature of Greek drama, there is no question that the ancient poet is more reticent and reserved in expression than the romantic dramatist would be in a similar situation. Take an illustration from the *Persae,* one of the earliest of the extant plays of Aeschylus, and pervaded with a lyrical spirit. This opens with a lengthy ode, in which the Persian elders recount the forces which took the field under Xerxes. In this narrative the descriptive element is utterly absent, and even when Atossa asks, "Where is Athens?" the Attic poet, who might well at this point have enlarged upon the beauty and picturesqueness of his native city, makes a reply almost as brief as the question. It is "far to the west, where sets our Lord the Sun."[6]

In Sophocles, the *Electra* and *Oedipus Tyrannus* are almost free from the descriptive or picturesque element, and even in the *Antigone,* when the heroine passes to her living tomb, she devotes only one short line to her loss of this beautiful world.[7] Even in Euripides, such plays as the *Heracleidae,* the *Hecuba,* and the *Andro-*

[6] *Persae,* 232. [7] *Antigone,* 879.

mache are singularly devoid of romantic coloring.

As we have seen in the case of the lyric poets, so, with the dramatic, single epithets are often deemed sufficient for description. These epithets may refer to merely material aspects. Thus in Aeschylus Argos is "deep soiled"[8] and has fertilizing streams";[9] Sicily is a land "of fair fruit,"[10] while the Nile is a "cattle-nurturing" stream,[11] "much-fostering,"[12] and has "outlets of fine sand."[13] In Euripides, Argos is a "thirsty" land,[14] Thrace is "buried in snow,"[15] Salamis is a "land of vines,"[16] and the rock of Sunium is "veined with silver."[17] This material aspect finds fuller expression in one of the fragments, where the poet is contrasting Laconia with Messenia. The former has "much corn-land, but it is hard to work. It is a valley, surrounded by mountains, rugged and inaccessible to the foe." Messenia is "rich in fruits, is watered by countless streams, and affords good pasture for flocks and herds. It is neither

[8] *Septem*, 306.
[9] *Suppliants*, 1028.
[10] *Prometheus*, 371.
[11] *Supp.* 855.
[12] *Persae*, 33.
[13] *Supp.* 3.
[14] *Alcestis*, 560.
[15] *Andromache*, 215.
[16] *Frag.*, 350.
[17] *Cyclops*, 294.

bleak and swept by winter's blasts, nor is it burnt with the heat from the sun's four steeds.[18]

A higher aesthetic tone is to be recognized in many passages where single epithets still suffice to meet the poet's needs. Thus the frequent use of adjectives implying a religious feeling, as when the sky or a river is called "pure," or "holy," and the earth or a grove is "divine." Similarly, there is the frequent use of adjectives describing the sun, day or water as "bright" or "clear." It is worth noting that expressions denoting splendor or brilliance are twice as common in Sophocles as in Aeschylus, and far more frequent and varied in Euripides than in either Aeschylus or Sophocles.[19]

The color range of the Greek tragedians makes an interesting study. *White* and *gray* occur in Euripides more than three times as often as in Aeschylus or Sophocles, while *black* is found in the seven plays of the sombre Aeschylus nearly as often as in the nineteen plays of Euripides, and between two and three times as often as in Sophocles. *Green,* so com-

[18] *Frag.*, 1083.
[19] Euripides uses λαμπρός and kindred words 66 times.

mon in Euripides, does not occur in Aeschylus, and is rare in Sophocles. *Red, yellow,* and *blue* are rare except in Euripides. *Purple,* however, a foreign color, is in comparative excess in Aeschylus, in whom there is an Oriental strain. It hardly occurs in Sophocles, but Euripides has ten instances.[20]

Thus it is obvious that Euripides has a distinctive feeling for color. He has a variety of terms to signify variations of hue, and in a number of passages he contrasts different colors. Thus in the *Helen,* the sympathetic attendant of the heroine heard her wailing when

> "I *was spreading, where grass droops trailing*
> I*n the river-flood's darkling gleam,*
> P*urple-dyed robes 'neath the blaze*
> O*f the sun, and his golden rays*
> O*verdraping the bulrush-sprays.*" [21]

In the Greek original of this passage four words denoting color are used. In the same play, the changing face of ocean is described by three color-terms, for the chorus pray that

[20] Details are given in the writer's essay on *The Attitude of the Greek Tragedians toward Nature,* Toronto, 1897.

[21] *Helen,* 179 ff. (A. S. Way).

Helen may be guided in safety across the light-blue swell of the sea, and across the white crest of the green-glimmering billows.[22]

As with most of the Greek poets, the love of nature in the tragedians is subordinate to other interests. Nature, for instance, may furnish lessons and illustrations for human life and conduct. Hence the frequent analogies drawn from sky and sea, from wind and storm, from plant and animal life. In Aeschylus the largest number of these come from the sea, and, as I have remarked elsewhere, if metaphors reflect the life of a people, the poetry of Aeschylus alone would suffice to prove that the Athenians lived half their life upon the ocean wave.[23] "Heaven laughs at the headstrong man as he fails to weather the cape. He wrecks forever his olden happiness on the reef of justice, and dies unwept, unseen." [24]

In Sophocles the idea that man has to bear joy and sorrow in constant succession finds an analogy in the movement of a heavenly constellation, for "grief and joy come round to

[22] *Helen,* 1501 ff. I have given Way's rendering of κυανόχροα as "green-glimmering," one of Swinburne's adjectives used of the sea.

[23] *The Attitude of the Greek Tragedians toward Nature,* p. 11.

[24] *Eumenides,* 560.

all, even as the Bear circles in his path."[25] So too nature teaches that man must be subject to fixed laws, for

> "*Dread potencies and powers*
> *Submit to law. Thus winter snow bestrown*
> *Gives place to opulent summer. Night's dim orb*
> *Is put to flight when Dawn with her white steeds*
> *Kindles the day-beams; and the wind's fierce breath*
> *Can lay the storm and lull the moaning deep,*
> . . . .
> *And we, shall we not likewise learn to yield?*"[26]

Sophocles too draws many of these illustrative pictures from the sea. Here is one that was doubtless suggested by a passage in the *Iliad:*[27]

> "*For as the tireless South or Northern blast*
> *Billow on billow rolls o'er ocean wide,*
> *So on the son of Cadmus follows fast*
> *Sea upon sea of trouble, tide on tide;*
> *And now he sinks, now rises; still some god*
> *Is nigh to save him from Death's whelming flood.*"[28]

Oedipus has known the stress of the storm:

[25] *Trachiniae,* 130.
[26] *Ajax,* 669 ff. (Storr).
[27] *Iliad,* II. 396 f.
[28] *Trachiniae,* 113 ff. (Storr).

"E'en *as some headland on an iron-bound shore,*
L*ashed by the wintry blasts and surge's roar,*
So *is he buffeted on every side*
B*y drear misfortune's whelming tide,*
B*y every wind of heaven o'erborne*
S*ome from the sunset, some from orient morn,*
S*ome from the noonday glow,*
S*ome from Rhipean gloom of everlasting snow.*"[29]

Similarly, Euripides takes many a lesson from the phenomena of nature. Here is a fine simile from the *Danaë:* "Of the same conditions, I maintain, as the fortunes of men is this ether, as we call it, whose qualities are these. In the summer it sends out a blaze of light, but in winter, gathering thick clouds, it swells the gloom. That all things bloom and fade, live and die, is due to this. So, too, with the seed of mortal men. Some enjoy a radiant calm, but for others again clouds gather; and some live on in the midst of evils, but others with all their wealth wane even as the changing seasons."[30]

But, as we may expect with an Attic poet, far the largest number of Euripides' illustrations come from the sea. The metaphor of a

[29] *Oedipus at Colonus,* 1240 ff. (Storr).
[30] *Frag.,* 330.

"sea of troubles" he uses many times.[31] Thebes is exposed to the billows of an Argive war,[32] and the Athenians, when in a hard plight, are like sailors, who having escaped the storm's rage are now close to land, yet are once more driven back by the winds into the deep.[33] A good friend is a more cheerful sight to one in trouble than a calm to sailors.[34]

"*Not among men doth fair fortune abide,*
But, as sail tempest-riven,
Is it whelmed in affliction's death-ravening tide
By the malice of heaven."[35]

Euripides can give a powerful description of a storm at sea, as in the *Troades*,[36] where Zeus sends his "rain and hail unspeakable and black tempests from heaven . . . and lightning fire," while Poseidon makes "the Aegean strait roar with great billows and whirlpools and fills Euboea's hollow bay with corpses," but he is more at home with ocean in her calmer moods, as when

[31] κακῶν πέλαγος, κῦμα, κλύδων, and similar expressions.
[32] *Phoenissae*, 859.
[33] *Heracleidae*, 427.
[34] *Orestes*, 727 f.
[35] *Ibid.* 340 ff. (Way).
[36] *Troades*, 78 ff.

"voice there is none, nor slumberous cheep
Of bird, nor whisper of sea; and deep
Is the hush of the winds on Euripus that sleep," [37]

or when "the breath of the winds is lost upon the deep, and Calm, child of Ocean, garbed in blue, cries thus: 'Be off! spread your sails to the breezes of the sea, and grasp your oars of pine, sailors, sailors, ho!'" [38]

Yet something of the heart's mad dance which the sailor feels when the gale blows strong, must surely have been felt by the poet who could thus sing of the mariner's elation, while laboring against an adverse wind: "the Tyrian main I left . . . and over the Ionian sea I plied the oar, for above the unharvested levels, skirting Sicily, raced the strong West Wind, sweetest music in the heavens." [39]

A study of the plant and animal life introduced into Greek tragedy shows how observant of nature were all these great poets, though Euripides has far the widest range, at least as regards the trees, fruits, and flowers of his native country. Here again external nature may illustrate human life. Aeschylus assigns

[37] *Iphigenia at Aulis,* 9 ff. (Way).
[38] *Helen,* 1455 ff.
[39] *Phoenissae,* 202 ff.

to Clytaemnestra a grim[40] comparison, when she likens the blood of her murdered husband to "the gentle rain from heaven." "As he breathes out a rapid tide of blood, he casts on me a dark drop of gory dew, while I exult no less than doth the corn, when beneath heaven's sweet rain the sheath bursts in labor."[41] In Sophocles, Ajax prays that his young son may be nurtured by gentle breezes, like a sapling,[42] and Deianeira describes her maidenhood under the same figure:

> "*Like to us, the tender plant*
> *Is reared and nurtured in some garden close;*
> *Nor heat, nor rain, nor any breath of air*
> *Vexes it, but unruffled, unperturbed,*
> *It buds and blossoms in sequestered bliss.*"[43]

Not a little of the beauty of Sophocles' famous ode on Colonus is due to the glory of flowers:

> "*And there, beneath the gentle dews of heaven,*
> *The fair narcissus with its clustered bells*
> *Blooms ever, day by day,*
> *Of old the wreath of mightiest Goddesses;*
> *And crocus golden-eyed.*"[44]

[40] Grim, but not grotesque, as Biese held in *Die Entwicklung des Naturgefühls bei den Griechen,* p. 39.
[41] *Agamemnon,* 1389.
[42] *Ajax,* 558.
[43] *Trachiniae,* 144 ff. (Storr).
[44] *Oedipus at Colonus,* 668 ff. (Plumptre).

Yet this is the only place in the extant plays of Sophocles where particular flowers are specified, and Aeschylus uses only their generic term. Euripides, however, indulges in considerable variety, for he has the rose, hyacinth, lotus-flower, and crocus. It was crocuses "with bloom of shimmering gold" that Creusa was plucking and gathering to her bosom, when golden-haired Apollo came to her.[45]

It is in Euripides too that we find the most numerous references to bright meadows, grassy glades, leafy coverts, forest glens, wild woodland, and mountain-thickets. Here, of course, as in all Greek poetry, we recognize the sphere of divinity, but the poet's love of nature thus finds suitable expression. To Hera belonged the meadow on Mount Cithaeron,[46] and Hippolytus crowned the spots "where the maiden Latona rested in the deep verdure."[47] It was to her he brought his wreath "culled from a virgin meadow, where no shepherd dares to feed his flock, and which the scythe has never entered, but the bee in spring-time wanders through that virgin meadow."[48]

Birds and beasts furnish abundant material

[45] *Ion,* 887 ff.
[46] *Phoenissae,* 24.
[47] *Hippolytus,* 1137.
[48] *Ibid.* 73.

for simile and metaphor to the dramatic poets. Of wild animals, the lion is conspicuous in Aeschylus and Euripides, but in all the dramatists domestic animals are more common, especially horses, cows, and bulls. Dogs and sheep are frequent in Euripides, who is also fond of stags and gazelles. The Danaid maiden of Aeschylus is "like a heifer that, chased by wolves, runs to and fro on steepy crags, and to the herdsman lows her tale of distress."[49] In Sophocles, the heifer may typify a girl of marriageable age.[50]

As to birds, Cassandra in Aeschylus is likened to a swan that sings most sweetly when dying.[51] She also wails sadly "like the tawny nightingale," but is far more unhappy. "The gods gave it a winged body, a pleasant and tearless life. For me there waits the stroke from two-edged sword."[52] In Sophocles, too, the nightingale, though "most musical" is also "most melancholy," as when the sighing of Electra is compared to its note of woe. Yet its "sightless song" is one of the glories of beautiful Colonus, the poet's birthplace:

49 *Suppliants,* 350.
50 *Trachiniae,* 530.
51 *Agamemnon,* 1444.
52 *Ibid.* 1141 ff.

"*But where we stand is surely holy ground,*
A wilderness of laurel, olive, vine;
Within a choir of songster nightingales
Are warbling."[53]

In Euripides, we find in some of his references to the lower creatures a peculiar tenderness that is quite Virgilian in tone and rare in Greek poetry. Andromache, robbed of noble Hector, is like a horse that has lost its yokefellow.[54] Megara guards the children of Heracles "as a hen keeps under her wings the chicks she has gathered in,"[55] and Polyxena is "like a calf reared on the hills" which its mother "will see torn from her, and sent to its death with severed throat."[56] So with birds. "I am loth to slay you," says Ion to the birds that haunt the temple, "but I must serve Phoebus."[57] Unhappy Electra, bewail-

[53] *Oedipus at Colonus,* 16 ff. (Storr). Cf. the familiar ode on Colonus, 670 ff.

"Where evermore, in thickets freshly green,
The clear-voiced nightingale
Still haunts, and pours her song,
By purpling ivy hid
And the thick leafage sacred to the God."
(Plumptre)

[54] *Troades,* 669; cf. Virgil, *Georgics,* III. 517.
[55] *Heracleidae,* 10; cf. *Andromache,* 441, *Troades,* 751.
[56] *Hecuba,* 205 ff.
[57] *Ion,* 179.

ing her father, is "like a clear-voiced swan beside the flowing river, calling to the loved parent bird, which is dying in a treacherous snare."[58]

The universal tendency of the Greeks to spiritualize and personify nature — a subject which we broached in an earlier chapter — may easily be illustrated from the tragedians. A modern poet might speak of a beautiful island washed by the sea, but Aeschylus tells us of an island fronting Salamis, upon whose "sea-washed shore dance-loving Pan is wont to tread."[59] It is Nature herself that sympathizes with the suffering Prometheus when the Ocean-Nymphs weep for him.[60] The splendid Bacchic hymn in Sophocles' *Antigone* is an excellent example of this mythological treatment of nature. The god "dwells by the soft streams of Ismenus," and is seen "above the twin peaks" of Parnassus, by the "torch-flames gleaming through smoke, where dance the Corycian nymphs, hard by the Castalian fount." He has come "from the ivy-mantled slopes of Nysa's hills, and the shore green with clustered vines." He is "leader of the stars,

58 *Electra,* 151.
59 *Persae,* 448 (Smyth).
60 *Prometheus,* 144.

whose breath is fire and master of the voices of the night." [61] So, too, "in the sanctity of his leafy grove at Colonus, which the sun never sees, and the stormy winds leave untouched, the reveller Dionysus ever treads the ground, ranging with the nymphs that nursed him. . . Nor has the Muses' choir abhorred this spot nor Aphrodite of the golden rein." [62]

But it is Euripides who gives us the most numerous illustrations of this feeling for nature disguised under the garb of mythology. "I come," says Poseidon in the opening of the *Troades*,

> "*Up from Aegean caverns, pool by pool*
> *Of blue salt sea, where feet most beautiful*
> *Of Nereïd maidens weave beneath the foam*
> *Their long sea-dances.*" [63]

As the Greek ships sail for Troy, they lead the Nereids in their dance, while the flute-loving dolphin leaps and rolls about the deep blue prows,[64] and a daring voyage into unknown waters calls forth these ringing verses: [65]

[61] *Antigone*, 1115–1152.
[62] *Oedipus at Colonus*, 668–719.
[63] *Troades*, 1 ff. (Gilbert Murray).
[64] *Electra*, 432 ff.
[65] *Iphigenia in Tauris*, 421–438 (Gilbert Murray).

"*Through the Clashing Rocks they burst:*
They passed by the Cape unsleeping
Of Phineus' sons accurst:
They ran by the star-lit bay
Upon magic surges sweeping,
Where folk on the waves astray
Have seen, through the gleaming grey,
Ring behind ring, men say,
The dance of the old Sea's daughters.

The guiding oar abaft
It rippled and it dinned,
And now the west wind laughed
And now the south-west wind;
And the sail was full in flight
And they passed by the Island White:

Birds, birds, everywhere,
White as the foam, light as the air;
And ghostly Achilles raceth there,
Far in the Friendless Waters."

Surely, notwithstanding Amphitrite and the Nereids, there is an almost Byronic spirit in these verses.

And where can one find a more vivid picture of sunrise than at the opening of the *Ion,* when the young ministrant in the temple chants these anapaests?

"Lo, *yonder the Sun-god is turning to earthward his splendour-blazing*
Chariot of light;
And the stars from the firmament flee from the fiery arrows chasing,
To the sacred night:
And the crests of Parnassus untrodden are flaming and flushed, as with yearning
Of welcome to far-flashing wheels with the glory of daylight returning
To mortal sight." [66]

Here surely we have the same lyric exaltation and mood that we find in Shelley's *Hymn of Apollo,* in William Blake's

"O *radiant morning, salute the Sun,*
Roused like a huntsman to the chase, and with
Thy buskined feet appear upon our hills,"

or even in Shakespeare's

"*Hark, hark! the lark at heaven's gate sings*
And Phoebus 'gins arise."

In this Ion passage the mythological garb is scanty, and in some scenes it is wholly cast aside, as when the Ajax in Sophocles bids farewell to familiar scenes,[67]

[66] *Ion,* 82 ff. (Way). [67] *Ajax,* 862 f. (Way).

"*Ye Trojan springs and streams, ye plains of Troy,*
Farewell, ye nurses of my fame, farewell!"

and gently chides them for deserting him,[68]

"*Paths of the roaring waves,*
Ye salt sea caves
And pastures by the shore,
Where long, too long I roam
In Troy-land, far from home;
Me shall ye see no more —
No more in life. Give ear
All who can hear.
Streams of Scamander, rills
That flow from Ida's hills,
Streams to the Greeks so dear,
Ne'er shall ye look on Ajax more."

It is in the *Philoctetes,* however, that in most striking fashion Sophocles has his hero yearn for the sympathy of the "familiar presences" of nature:

"*Ye creeks, ye promontories, dens and lairs*
Of mountain beasts, ye cliffs precipitous,
To you — none else will heed me — I appeal,
On you, familiars of my woes, I call."[69]

When Neoptolemus and Odysseus leave him to his fate, he turns in helpless appeal to the cave that had sheltered him so long:

68 *Ajax,* 412 ff. (Way). 69 *Philoctetes,* 936 ff. (Way).

"O *cavern'd rock, my cell*
Now hot, now icy chill,
How long with thee it was my lot to dwell:
To thee till death I shall be constant still;" [70]

and later, when he leaves his island home, he thus bids it a loving farewell:

"*Home of my vigils, rocky cell,*
Nymphs of the streams and grass-fringed shore,
Caves where the deep-voiced breakers roar,
When through the cavern's open mouth,
Borne on the wings of the wild South,
E'en to my dwelling's inmost lair,
The rain and spray oft drenched my hair;
And oft responsive to my groan
Mount Hermaeum made his moan;
O Lycian fount, O limpid well,
I thought with you all time to dwell;
And now I take my last farewell." [71]

The "responsive moan" of the mountain in this moving passage, and the ceaseless "beating of the surge around" [72] the suffering hero, sounding that "eternal note of sadness," which Matthew Arnold found in Sophocles,[73] bring us into that atmosphere of feeling which has been called the "pathetic fallacy." Rus-

[70] *Philoctetes,* 1081 ff.
[71] *Ibid.* 1453 ff.
[72] *Ibid.* 689.
[73] *Dover Beach.*

kin[74] is right in assuming that this attitude is rare in Greek poetry, while frequent in modern, for the modern poet is commonly steeped in the self-conscious, introspective spirit that transfers man's joys and sorrows to inanimate nature.

> "*We receive but what we give,*
> *And in our life alone does nature live;*
> *Ours is her wedding-garment, ours her shroud.*"[75]

Keats, who is so thoroughly Greek in his way of looking upon the external world, is remarkably free from the pathetic fallacy,[76] and recently a critic has said of our American poet, Robert Frost: "He spends no time dilating on the aloofness or indifference of nature to man." "Frost's poetry contains no taint of the 'pathetic fallacy' of the romanticist, which in these days is almost sufficient ground for suspecting Frost's classical tendencies."[77]

In Aeschylus the nearest approach to pathetic fallacy is in the *Prometheus*, where the tortured soul pours out his immortal appeal to

[74] *Modern Painters*, Pt. IV, Ch. 12.
[75] Coleridge.
[76] See *Studies in Interpretation*, by W. H. Hudson, New York, 1896.
[77] *Robert Frost, A Study in Sensibility and Good Sense*, by Gorham B. Munson, New York, 1927.

Nature, who is his sole witness, and who alone can sympathize with him in suffering:

"O *Holy Aether, and swift-winged Winds,*
And River-wells, and Laughter innumerous
Of yon sea-waves! Earth, mother of us all,
And all-viewing cyclic Sun, I cry on you,—
Behold me a god, what I endure from gods!" [78]

So too all Nature sympathizes with the Titan Atlas in his anguish: "the waves of ocean murmur as they sink in cadence, the deep laments, the black pit of Hades' land rumbles in accord, and the fountains of pure-flowing rivers lament the piteous pain." [79] It has been observed that, though invested with a thoroughly human interest, Prometheus and Atlas are yet superhuman beings, and it is significant that only in these two cases can we detect the pathetic fallacy in Aeschylus. In Sophocles we have already encountered some interesting examples, but it is in Euripides that, among tragic poets, we find the most numerous instances of this transfer of human emotion to external nature.

"*Ah, alas for the sands of the shore!*
Alas for the brakes of the hill,

[78] *Prometheus,* 88 ff. (Elizabeth Barrett Browning).
[79] *Prometheus,* 431 ff. If the preceding lines, 425–430, are an interpolation, as Smyth holds, following Badham, the passage cited refers to Prometheus, not Atlas.

Where the wolves shall fear thee no more,
And thy cry to Dictynna is still!" [80]

Thus cries the chorus in the *Hippolytus.* In the *Tauric Iphigenia,* the captive Greek women sorrow with the halcyon, ever moaning for its mate: [81]

"*Bird of the sea-rocks, of the bursting spray,*
O halcyon bird,
That wheelest crying, crying, on thy way;
Who knoweth grief can read the tale of thee:
One love long lost, one song for ever heard
And wings that sweep the sea."

Conversely, the mother on recovering her lost son pours out her joy to "bright heaven's expanses," [82] and the aged Thebans, when freed from terror, break forth into these exultant strains: [83]

"*Deck thee with garlands, Ismenus, and ye*
Break forth into dancing,
Streets stately with Thebes' fair masonry
And Dirce bright-glancing:

Come, Maids of Asopus, to us, from the spring
Come ye of your father;

[80] *Hippolytus,* 1126 ff. (Gilbert Murray).
[81] *Iphigenia in Tauris,* 1089 ff. (Gilbert Murray).
[82] *Ion,* 1445.
[83] *The Mad Hercules,* 781 ff. (Way).

Of Hercules' glorious triumph to sing,
Nymph-chorus, O gather.

Pythian forest-peak, Helicon's steep
Of the Song-queens haunted,
To my town, to my walls, let the song-echoes leap
Of the strains loud-chanted."

The joyous bridegroom in the *Helen* would have "the whole earth raise in happy melody his wedding-song," [84] and in a similar spirit Evadne in the *Suppliants* recalls her marriage-day:

"*Where now that light that shone*
When flashed thy wheels, O Sun,
Or when the moon raced on,
And star-lamps glancing
Raced through a lowering sky,
When Argos tossed on high
The gladsome bridal-cry,
And throbbed with dancing,
And thrilled with song, to see
Mine hero wed with me?"-[85]

In the joyous Eleusinian festival even the elements unite with mortals in the solemn worship,

[84] *Helen*, 1433.   [85] *Suppliants*, 990 ff. (Way).

"*When dances heaven star-glancing*
Adoringly,
When the white moon is dancing,
And 'neath the sea
The Nereids' dance enrings
The eternal river-springs,
And their full chorus sings Persephonê
Gold-crowned, and our Earth-mother." [86]

Here, for a moment, we have man and nature in perfect accord, but in the *Bacchae,* which is fundamentally a mystical nature-drama, we have that accord throughout the play. "The whole land will dance" with joy; "with milk flows the earth, with wine and honey's nectar, and a smoke arises as of Syrian incense." The Bacchantes sleep in security where they will, on pine branches or oak leaves in the forest. They "gird themselves with snakes, that lick their cheeks. Some fondle in their arms gazelles or savage whelps of wolves and give them suck. Others crown their heads with ivy or oak or blossoming smilax, and one taking her thyrsus strikes it into the rock and straightway there leaps forth a dewy stream of water. Another plunges her wand into the earth's soil and there the god sends up a fount of wine, and

[86] *Ion,* 1078 ff. (Way).

all who wish for the white fluid, with finger-tips scratch the soil and get them milk in streams, while from their wands, with ivy wreathed, sweet rills of honey trickle." When the Bacchantes wave their wands and call in loud chorus upon their god, at once "the whole mountain joined in the Bacchic cry, the wild beasts answered and all nature was stirred."[87] And lastly there is that marvellous description of the sudden lull in the voices of nature just before nature's god breaks out in his storm of wrath:

"*Hushed was the welkin; all the forest-glade*
Held hushed its leaves; no wild thing's cry was
heard."[88]

There is probably no poem in the world's literature in which man and nature are in closer sympathy than in this great work of art, the *Bacchae* of Euripides.

"*But O for the land that in beauty is peerless,*[89]
The Pierian haunt where the Muses sing!
On Olympus the hallowed to stand all fearless
Thitherward lead me, O Clamour-king!
O Revel-god, guide where the Graces abide

[87] *Bacchae,* 115, 142 f., 684 f., 698 ff., 725 f.
[88] *Bacchae,* 1084 f. (Way).
[89] Macedonia, where the play was composed.

And Desire,—where danceth, of no man denied,
The Bacchanal ring." [90]

Euripides indeed, as judged by the prevailing standards of his day was a sentimentalist, and I am convinced that the hostility of Aristophanes to the poet was due, in no small measure, to the latter's attitude toward nature. The *Bacchae* was composed far away from the conventional life of Athens, in a country where the poet could give free rein to his romantic spirit and love for the beauty of nature unadorned. Even in other plays, however, we may detect the same note, the longing for an escape to open spaces, the call of the wild, which is a commonplace thought in our modern poetry. Here are two examples from Jean Ingelow: [91]

"O, *to be a wild white bird, and seek thy rocky bed!"*

"O, *to be at least a cloud, that near thee I might flow!"*

So in the *Hippolytus*, Phaedra cries:

"*Oh for a deep and dewy spring,*
With runlets cold to draw and drink!
And a great meadow blossoming

[90] *Bacchae,* 409 ff. (Way).
[91] Jean Ingelow, *Requiescat in Pace!*

Long-grassed, and poplars in a ring,
To rest me by the brink!" [92]

whereupon she is rebuked by her nurse for blurting out such frenzied words in public — the rebuke, as Professor Sandys observes, probably giving us a clue to the feeling of the ordinary Athenian of the day upon such matters. But longing for solitude and distant places is not infrequent elsewhere in this poet. Thus in the *Helen,* the chorus cry:

"*Oh through the welkin on pinions to fleet*
Where from Libya far-soaring
The cranes by their armies flee fast from the sleet
And the storm-waters pouring." [93]

So too Creusa, in the *Ion:* [94]

"*Oh to flee on the wings of a bird*
Through the ocean of air and from Hellas afar to the stars of the west!"

and Antigone, in the *Phoenissae:* [95]

"O *that as wind-driven clouds swift-racing,*
I *might speed with my feet through the air,"*

and Electra in the *Orestes:* [96]

[92] *Hippolytus,* 208 ff. (Gilbert Murray).
[93] *Helen,* 1477 ff. (Way).
[94] *Ion,* 796 f. (Way).
[95] *Phoenissae,* 163 f. (Way).
[96] *Orestes,* 982 ff. (Way).

"O *might I win to the rock 'twixt heaven*
And earth suspended in circles swinging,
Upborne by the golden chains scarce-clinging,
The shard from Olympus riven!" [97]

But the most daring of these imaginative flights is found in another of the choral songs of the *Hippolytus*,[98] where the simple theme, "Would that I were a bird!" is grandly amplified through strophe and antistrophe, and the bird's flight takes us over the Adriatic to the River Po, to the region of amber, to the Gardens of the Hesperides, and then to "that Pillar of the End that Atlas guardeth,"

"*Where a voice of living waters never ceaseth*
In God's quiet garden by the sea,
And Earth, the ancient life-giver, increaseth
Joy among the meadows, like a tree."

Thus Euripides abounds in the romantic sentiment toward nature, and in this respect no Greek poet approaches him until we come to Theocritus. Especially does Euripides resemble Theocritus in a certain naïve and idyllic

[97] A reference to Anaxagoras, who held that the sun was a mass of fiery stone held in suspense.

[98] *Hippolytus*, 732 ff. (Gilbert Murray). In this, as in most of his free renderings of choral songs, Murray, himself a genuine poet, catches the spirit of a highly poetical passage.

tone, which well suits the pastoral atmosphere of the satyric drama, the *Cyclops,* but is also characteristic of certain tragedies, notably the *Ion* and the *Iphigenia at Aulis.* In one of the songs of the *Andromache,* Hermes leads the three goddesses to the fold of the shepherd Paris:

> " *For the strife to the steadings of herds did they come,*
> *To the stripling shepherd in solitude biding,*
> *And the hearth of the lodge in the forest lone.*
>
> *They have passed 'neath the leaves of the glen: from the plashing*
> *Of the mountain-spring radiant in rose-flush they rise,"* [99]

and in the *Iphigenia at Aulis,* the song is addressed to Paris:

> " *Thou camest, Paris, back to where,*
> *Mid Ida's heifers snowy fair,*
> *A neatherd, thou didst pipe such strain*
> *That old Olympus's spirit there*
> *Awoke again.*
> *Full-uddered kine in dreamy peace*
> *Browsed, when the summons came to thee."* [100]

[99] *Andromache,* 279 ff. (Way).
[100] *Iphigenia at Aulis,* 573 ff. (Way).

As for the doubtful *Rhesus*, I long ago[101] expressed my belief that it is a genuine work by Euripides, and I am glad to find my view confirmed by Professor Gilbert Murray, to whom, as to me, "the lines about the Nightingale in the 'Watcher's Song' speak for Euripides": [102]

> "*Nay, hearken! Again she is crying,*
> *Where death-laden Simois falls,*
> *Of the face of dead Itys that stunned her,*
> *Of grief grown to music and wonder:*
> *Most changeful and old and undying*
> *The nightingale calls.*
>
> *And on Ida the shepherds are waking*
> *Their flocks for the upland. I hear*
> *The skirl of a pipe very distant.*
>
> *And sleep, it falls slow and insistent.*
> *'Tis perilous sweet when the breaking*
> *Of dawn is so near.*" [103]

From the point of view of our present study, Euripides is the most conspicuous figure in all Greek literature. He loves nature as a subject of primary interest, and revels in the glories of the heavens above, and of his earthly para-

[101] *The Attitude of the Greek Tragedians toward Nature*, p. 66.
[102] *The Rhesus of Euripides*, Gilbert Murray, p. x f.
[103] *Rhesus*, 546 ff. (Gilbert Murray).

dise here below. Like Pindar, he delights in brilliance and color, but he goes far beyond Pindar in personalizing nature and endowing her with a life and spirit of her own, so that, almost for the first time in Greek poetry, we can have sympathy between man and nature expressed in terms of modern nature-poetry. Perhaps no single passage will illustrate this better than a glorious choral song of Bacchantes as beautifully rendered by Gilbert Murray, who unlike most verse translators, pays homage to the poetry of the original by giving us, as an equivalent, a genuine English poem:

"Will they ever come to me, ever again,
The long, long dances,
On through the dark till the dim stars wane?
Shall I feel the dew on my throat, and the stream
Of wind in my hair? Shall our white feet gleam
In the dim expanses?
Oh, feet of a fawn to the greenwood fled,
Alone in the grass and the loveliness;
Leap of the hunted, no more in dread,
Beyond the snares and the deadly press:
Yet a voice still in the distance sounds,
A voice and a fear and a haste of hounds;
O wildly labouring, fiercely fleet,

Onward yet by river and glen. . .
Is it joy or terror, ye storm-swift feet? . . .
To the dear lone lands untroubled of men.
Where no voice sounds, and amid the shadowy green
The little things of the woodland live unseen.

What else is Wisdom? What of man's endeavour
Or God's high grace, so lovely and so great?
To stand from fear set free, to breathe and wait;
To hold a hand uplifted over Hate;
And shall not Loveliness be loved for ever?" [104]

"Greek poetry," says Gilbert Murray in one of his essays,[105] "is never far removed from the primitive religious dance." In the *Bacchae,* at least, the poet is very close to the spirit of nature.

This is not the place to discuss in detail the well-known hostility of Aristophanes toward Euripides, as shown most vividly in the *Frogs.* In this comedy, which was first exhibited in 405 B.C., the very year of the first presentation of the posthumous *Bacchae,* Aristophanes makes merry with the "twitterings" of the

[104] *Bacchae,* 862 ff. (Gilbert Murray).
[105] *Essays and Studies by Members of the English Association,* Vol. III, p. 30, Oxford, 1912.

dead tragedian in amusing parodies, the most obvious feature of which, I take it, is exaggerated and affected sentiment, illustrated by minute and toying descriptions of external nature. "O darkly-light mysterious Night" gives the keynote of Euripidean monodies, while the prevailing spirit of the tragic writer's lyrics is set forth in a composite picture of halcyons chattering by the sea-waves, spiders spinning their webs, dolphins sporting under the blue prows of ships, all mixed up with vines and grapes — surely the themes of a nature-poet, though thrown together in comic and incongruous fashion:

"*Halcyons, who by the ever-rippling*
Waves of the sea are babbling,
Dewing your plumes with the drops that fall
From wings in the salt spray dabbling.

Spiders ever with twir-r-r-r-rling fingers
Weaving the warp and the woof,
Little, brittle, network, fretwork,
Under the coigns of the roof.

The minstrel shuttle's care.

Where in the front of the dark-prowed ships
Yarely the flute-loving dolphin skips

Races here and oracles there.

And the joy of the young vines smiling,
And the tendril of grapes, care-beguiling." [106]

And yet, elsewhere, Aristophanes betrays himself as a lyric poet of the highest rank, who in later days was known as " the darling of the Graces." Listen to the frogs themselves:

" *Loud and louder our chant must flow.*
Sing if ever ye sang of yore,
When in sunny and glorious days
Through the rushes and marsh-flags springing
On we swept, in the joy of singing
Myriad-diving roundelays.
Or when fleeing the storm, we went
Down to the depths, and our choral song
Wildly raised to a loud and long
Bubble-bursting accompaniment." [107]

And surely something of the spirit of a Shelley is revealed in the song of the clouds:

" *Clouds of all hue,*
Rise we aloft with our garments of dew.
Come from old Ocean's unchangeable bed,
Come, till the mountain's green summits we tread,
Come to the peaks with their landscapes untold,
Gaze on the Earth with her harvests of gold,

[106] Aristophanes, *Frogs*, 1309–1331 (Rogers' translation).
[107] *Frogs*, 241 ff. (Rogers).

Gaze on the rivers in majesty streaming,
Gaze on the lordly invincible Sea,
Come, for the Eye of the Ether is beaming,
Come, for all Nature is flashing and free.
Let us shake off this close-clinging dew
From our members eternally new,
And sail upwards the wide world to view.
Come away! Come away!" [108]

and in the hoopoo's call to the nightingale:

"*Wake, Mistress, wake, from slumber cease,*
The strains of sacred song release,
The dirge that from thy lips divine
Pours forth for Itys, thine and mine,
The liquid melody that thrills
Thy golden throat.
Through leaf-tressed briony thy cry
Uprises clear to Zeus on high,
Where golden-haired Apollo hears,
And straight responsive to thy tears,
His ivory lyre Olympus fills
With dulcet note.
Then, as they tread the dance's maze,
The gods upraise
In unison their holy lays." [109]

It is because of such lyric songs interspersed among the laughter-raising comedies that

[108] *Clouds,* 275 ff. (Rogers).
[109] *Birds,* 209 ff. (Marshall MacGregor).

Swinburne regards Aristophanes as a "half-divine humourist in whose incomparable genius the highest qualities of Rabelais were fused and harmonized with the supremest gifts of Shelley." [110]

[110] Swinburne, in his preface to "*Grand Chorus of Birds from Aristophanes.*"

VIII. THE ALEXANDRIAN AND LATER AGES

(THEOCRITUS AND THE ANTHOLOGY)

Return, Alpheus, the dread voice is past,
That shrunk thy streams; return, Sicilian Muse.[1]

MILTON

And, O Theocritus, . .
I hear thee tell how bees with honey fed
Divine Comates, by his impious lord
Within a chest imprisoned; how they came
Laden from blooming grove or flowery field
And fed him there, alive, month after month,
Because the goatherd, blessed man! had lips
Wet with the Muses' nectar.[2] WORDSWORTH

Theocritus, with glittering locks
Dropt sideways, as betwixt the rocks
He watched the visionary flocks.[3]

ELIZABETH BARRETT BROWNING

I should be content to die, if I had written anything equal to this.[4] TENNYSON

Like Theocritus, Tennyson finds in nature and in legends of past ages subjects congenial to his muse. *Oenone* and

[1] Milton, *Lycidas*.
[2] Wordsworth, *The Prelude,* Book XI, fin.
[3] *A Vision of Poets*.
[4] *Memoir,* vol. II, p. 495. Said of the *Hylas* Idyll of Theocritus.

Tithonus are steeped in the golden beauty of Syracusan art.[5] JOHN ADDINGTON SYMONDS

O singer of the field and fold,
Theocritus! Pan's pipe was thine —
Thine was the happier Age of Gold.

AUSTIN DOBSON

Poetry in Mr. Frost exhibits almost the identical desires and impulses we see in the "bucolic" poems of Theocritus.[6]

THE NATION

The younger American singers, whatever their merits, have paid more tributes to Theocritus than to any other ancient poet.[7] ROBERT THOMAS KERLIN

Somewhat, Theocritus, thou hast to answer for, thou that first of men brought the shepherd to Court, and made courtiers wild to go a Maying with the shepherds.[8]

ANDREW LANG

The lambs did play, the grounds were green,
The trees did bud, the zun did sheen;
The lark did zing below the sky,
An' roads wer all a-blown so dry,
As if the zummer wer begun.[9] WILLIAM BARNES

Euterpe, since they brought to you the long
unbroken centuries of Grecian song,
after another thousand years, I bring
these English echoes, and, though faltering,
will you, because I dare not, offer these
to Meleager and Simonides.[10] HUMBERT WOLFE

[5] *The Greek Poets,* vol. II. p. 290.
[6] Cited by Gorham B. Munson, in *Robert Frost,* p. 120.
[7] *Theocritus in English Literature,* 1910, p. 165.
[8] *Letters to Dead Authors,* p. 139.
[9] Barnes, *Poems of Rural Life* ("Easter Zunday").
[10] *Others Abide,* 1928 (Invocation).

THE CITY of Alexandria was founded in 331 B.C., and this capital of the new Ptolemaic kingdom of Egypt soon vied with Athens as the intellectual centre of the Greek world. The most distinguished men of letters and learning were invited to the court of the Ptolemies, and the new Library and Museum of Alexandria became for the ancient world the nearest equivalent of a great modern University seat of learning.

All of the Alexandrian librarians were scholars and writers, and included three great Homeric critics, Zenodotus, Aristophanes of Byzantium, and Aristarchus, as well as Eratosthenes the encyclopedist, and the two rival poets, Callimachus and Apollonius. These poets, both born about a century after the death of Euripides, are worthy of notice in connection with our theme. All the prose writings of Callimachus are lost and several of his poems as well. One of these, however, the *Lock of Berenice,* has survived in the translation of Catullus, while the *Ibis* is probably echoed in the *Ibis* of Ovid. As to the lost *Causes,* it was a source of much mythological material for the Roman elegists, and both

Martial and Ovid speak, the one of its learned, the other of its sentimental character. The surviving poems include six hymns, sixty-three epigrams, and fragments of an epic, the *Hecale*, first published as recently as 1893.

The *Hymn to Delos* is a good specimen of the poet's art and thought. It involves an elaborate personification of the island of Delos, and indeed many lands, islands, mountains, and rivers are freely personified, and we are carried back to the atmosphere of the old Homeric hymns, which served as a model for Callimachus.

The river Peneus was ready to shelter the wandering Leto, soon to become mother of Apollo, but Ares, in league with Hera, threatened to throw the peaks of Pangaeus into his waters, and blot out his streams. "And the hills of Ossa trembled, and the plain of Crannon, and the windswept skirts of Pindus, and all Thessaly danced for fear."[11] Cos, "the isle of Merops," might have become the god's birthplace, but Apollo himself, speaking from his mother's womb, begged her not to bear him in Cos, for "there is due to the island from

[11] Callimachus, *Hymn* IV. 137 ff. (A. W. Mair's translation in *The Loeb Classical Library*, 1921).

the Fates another god, the most high lineage of the Saviours,"[12] but to carry him to the floating island Asteria, henceforth to be known to seafaring men as Delos, the island no longer obscure (*a-delos*).[13] Here, at the moment of birth, the nymphs of the isle, "sang with far-sounding voice the holy chant of Eileithyia. And straightway the brazen sky echoed back the far-reaching chant and Hera grudged it not, because Zeus had taken away her anger. In that hour, O Delos, all thy foundations became of gold: with gold thy round lake flowed all day, and golden foliage thy natal olive-tree put forth and with gold flowed coiled Inopus in deep flood."[14]

Here we have illustrations of two features of "Alexandrianism"—its learning, not to say pedantry, and its exaggeration of thought and expression. The derivation of a geographical term comes as a painful surprise, and though in early literature we are pleased by the natural and spontaneous personification of mountains, rivers, and other aspects of nature, we feel that in the late and sophisticated age

[12] i.e. Ptolemy Philadelphus, son of Ptolemy Soter, who was born in Cos in 310 B.C.
[13] *Hymn* IV. 51–54; 160–166.
[14] *Ibid.* 255–263.

which we have reached such an attitude may be largely imitative and artificial, especially if maintained through a poem of three hundred and twenty-six verses. Hence we are not moved very sympathetically even when Callimachus has his altars heaped up with varied flowers in spring and with crocuses in winter; [15] when the red blush mounted up on Pallas, "as the colour of the morning rose or seed of pomegranate"; [16] when the sea is hushed, as the minstrels sing Phoebus; [17] when the rock of Niobe withholds its tears of pain; [18] or when Artemis, having asked Zeus for mountains, and received both mountains and many cities, pays a visit to the Cyclopes, whom she found fashioning a horse-trough (!) for Poseidon, and at the great blast of the bellows and the groaning of the smiths "Aetna cried aloud, and Trinacria cried, the seat of the Sicanians, cried too their neighbor Italy, and Cyrnos uttered a mighty noise." [19]

And yet Callimachus has seen the god of light and learning, and "whoso hath seen

[15] Callimachus, *Hymn* II. 80 ff.
[16] *Ibid. Hymn* V. 27 f. (Mair).
[17] *Ibid. Hymn* II. 18 f.
[18] *Ibid. Hymn* II. 22 ff.
[19] *Ibid. Hymn* III. 18–58 (Mair).

Apollo, he is great; whoso hath not seen him, he is of low estate."[20]

Apollonius is much superior in poetic genius to his older rival, and his *Argonautica* is an epic of no mean rank. He is very erudite, it is true, but he is also more truly inspired, and more bound by the spell of earlier literature, notably that of Homer. The palace of Aeetes, built by Hephaestus,[21] recalls that of Alcinous, but is even more sumptuous. The poet's similes are numerous and Homeric, but often more detailed, and the Argonauts have adventures in lands of mystery which rival those of Odysseus himself. Orpheus' song of creation is a Hesiodic strain, and worthy of comparison with its famous offspring, Virgil's song of Silenus in the Sixth *Eclogue*.[22]

In his beautiful essay on *the Dawn of Romanticism in Greek Poetry,* Professor Butcher has called our attention to some characteristics of Apollonius. We have, of course, for the first time romantic love made the chief feature of an epic, but we also have in this poet "a modern spirit in his descriptive art. He is

[20] Callimachus, *Hymn* II. 10 (Mair).
[21] *Argonautica,* III. 215–248.
[22] *Argonautica,* I. 496–511.

profoundly sensitive to the effects of air and light." [23] Thus, as gleaming Dawn with shining eyes looks upon the mountain peaks, the sea is ruffled by the wind.[24] As the sun passes the meridian, the poet notes how the shadows begin to creep from the rocks over the ploughlands,[25] and, as Jason lifts up the golden fleece, and the shimmering of the woolen flocks lights up his cheeks and brow with a red flush, he is reminded of a maiden who in her high-roofed chamber "catches on her finely wrought robe the gleam of the moon at its full." [26] When after the wedding of Jason and Medea, "Dawn, returning with her beams divine, scattered the gloomy night through the sea," then "the island beaches laughed out and the paths over the plains far off, drenched with dew, and there was a din in the streets." [27] When the lovers first met, they "stood face to face without a word, without a sound, like oaks or lofty pines, which stand quietly side by side on the mountains when the wind is still; then again, when

[23] Butcher, *Some Aspects of the Greek Genius* (3d Ed.) p. 300.

[24] *Argonautica,* I. 519 ff.

[25] *Ibid.* 450.

[26] *Ibid.* IV. 167 ff. (R. C. Seaton transl., in *The Loeb Classical Library,* 1912.)

[27] *Ibid.* 1170 ff. (Seaton).

stirred by the breath of the wind, they murmur ceaselessly." [28]

These are all apt and beautiful comparisons, but occasionally one has reason to suspect over-refinement. Though "the wavelets of dancing light cast on the walls from a vessel of water" give a pretty picture, it seems rather extravagant to compare with them the quiverings of a maiden's heart.[29] Again, as warriors spring up from the seed of the dragon's teeth, they are like hosts of stars shining through the gloom, "when abundant snow has fallen on the earth and the storm blasts have dispersed the wintry clouds under the murky night." [30] But what has the abundant snow to do with these shining warriors, for whose peers we are to look to the stars in heaven? The snowy earth makes us look down, not up.

Another poet of the Alexandrian age who deserves a word of notice is Aratus, whose astronomical poem, the *Phaenomena*, opens with the famous sentence: "From Zeus let us begin; him do we mortals never leave unnamed; full of Zeus are all the streets and all the market-places of men; full is the sea and

[28] *Argonautica,* III. 967 ff. (Seaton).
[29] *Ibid.* III. 755 ff. also Butcher, *op. cit.*, p. 302.
[30] *Ibid.* III. 1359 ff. (Seaton).

the havens thereof; always we all have need of Zeus. For we are also his offspring."[31] The first words of this passage have often been quoted in subsequent secular literature, and the last words are universally familiar through their citation by St. Paul before the Areopagus.

The poem, a versified rendering of a prose treatise by the mathematician Eudoxus, is a characteristic product of a learned age, being merely didactic and wholly devoid of those qualities which make the *Georgics* of Virgil, notwithstanding the unpromising material, thoroughly genuine poetry. Such interest in nature as the poem reveals should probably be credited to Eudoxus, whose work was composed as a scientific manual.

Another characteristic poem of the Alexandrian age survives in the extraordinary *Alexandra* of Lycophron. This iambic monody of nearly fifteen hundred verses is the work of an erudite versifier, and has been called "the most obscure production of Greek literature, a *tour de force* of cryptic language."[32] The poem is not wholly devoid of interest for us, but the

[31] *Phaenomena,* 1–5 (G. R. Mair's translation, in *The Loeb Classical Library,* 1921.)

[32] W. C. Wright, *A Short History of Greek Literature,* p. 445.

writer's concern with the beauties of nature is severely limited to brief similes or metaphors, and to slight, often monosyllabic descriptions of places associated with the fictions of mythology or the dreams of prophecy.

To turn from Lycophron and Aratus, or even from Callimachus and Apollonius, to Theocritus, is like opening the window of a hot, stuffy room to breathe the cool, refreshing air of the out-of-doors. That Theocritus should have been an Alexandrian has always been something of a puzzle, and indeed his remarkable freshness and naturalism have served to obscure the fact that even in Theocritus we can find too much of the artificiality, affectation, and insincerity of the age in which he lived. Theocritus wrote Pastorals and Mimes, but he also wrote a pattern- or figure-poem, the *Syrinx,* clever Epigrams, including a bank-advertisement,[33] Epyllia or Little Epics, and Encomia. These last are modelled upon the Homeric *Hymns,* and the Seventeenth Idyll is a fulsome and offensive eulogy of Ptolemy

[33] Epigram XIV (*Palatine Anthology,* 9.435) is treated in an article on *Bank Advertisements: Ancient and Modern,* by Charles J. Bullock, Professor of Economics in Harvard University. This appeared in *Barron's,* July 30, 1928.

Philadelphus. This opens, in the very words of the *Phaenomena* of Aratus, with an invocation to Zeus,[34] and closes with a reference to the same god. Cos, birthplace of Ptolemy, is elaborately personified, and handled in the same manner as was Delos, birthplace of Apollo, by Callimachus.[35] "And Cos did foster thee when thou wert still a child new-born, and received thee at thy mother's hand, when thou saw'st thy first dawning. . . And Cos brake forth into a cry, . . and touching the child with kind hands, she said: 'Blessed, O child, mayst thou be, and me mayst thou honour even as Phoebus Apollo honours Delos of the azure crown, yea, establish in the same renown the Triopean hill, and allot such glory to the Dorians dwelling nigh, as that wherewithal Prince Apollo favours Rhenaea.'"[36] Ptolemy's great dominion is described in arithmetical, supposedly mystical, terms, and after making a computation we learn that it embraced thirty-three thousand three hundred and three cities. And this god on earth, whose wife Arsinoe is his own sister, *Iovisque et soror*

[34] See p. 158 above.
[35] See p. 154 above.
[36] Theocritus, *Idyll* XVII, 58–70 (Andrew Lang)

et coniunx, enjoys a wedded bliss, like that of Zeus, whose bride was his sister Hera!

But these amazing indiscretions are quite forgotten, as we become immersed in the Idylls of town- and country-life, the Mimes and Pastorals. The Little Epics, too, are full of beauty, and it was the touching story of the youth Hylas in the Thirteenth Idyll, whose loss, when he was carried off by the water-nymphs, brought deep grief to Heracles, that aroused the intense admiration of Tennyson, mentioned on p. 150 above. The landscape setting for the scene is romantic, and much richer than in any earlier Greek poetry: [37]

"A *brazen pitcher swings in his hand, and soon he espied*
A *tarn in a lowly dell; thick rushes about it grew,*
The *swallow-wort's purple bell and maiden-hair pale of hue,*
And *parsley lush and fair and many a marsh-born thing."*

But the age-old belief in the spiritual presences of nature is also there, for

"In *the midst of the water there the nymphs were gambolling,*

[37] *Ibid. Idyll.* XIII. 39–52 (J. H. Hallard, London, 1924).

Sleepless naiads three, whom the awe-struck yokel flies,
Malis and Eunice, and Nychaea with Spring in her eyes."

He cannot escape them:

" *and into the dark pool there*
Headlong down slipped he, as a red star slips from the sky
Headlong into the sea — and the mariner will cry:
' Ho, lads! shorten sail, for a stiff breeze soon will blow.' "

Here again, as in Aeschylus and Euripides, we recognize Greek familiarity with the sea and sailor-life, a familiarity even more strikingly shown in the Twenty-first Idyll, the " Fishermen," which, however, is probably not by Theocritus, but perhaps by his contemporary, Leonidas of Tarentum. It is of this Idyll that Andrew Lang has written: " There is nothing in Wordsworth more real, more full of the incommunicable sense of nature. . . It is as true to nature as the statue of the naked fisherman in the Vatican. One cannot read these verses but the vision returns to one, of sand-hills by the sea, of a low cabin roofed with grass, where fishing-rods of reed are leaning against the door, while the Mediterranean floats up her waves that fill the waste with sound." [38]

In his Mimes, or town-life sketches, Theocritus shows that he has all the gifts needed by a romantic dramatist. His Second Idyll is a tale of passionate love, ending in utter despair, a deserted woman pouring out her pitiful story to the Moon, in the silence of night, and her terrible distress being made the more poignant by contrast with the beautiful but unfeeling calm of nature,

> "*Lo, now the winds and seas asleep are laid,*
> *But my heart's ache sleeps not and is not stayed,*" [39]

and this contrast is again and again enforced by the refrain,

> "*List, good Moon, where I learnt my loving.*" [40]

To Simaetha, the Moon was her only possible comfort. Is it far-fetched to compare with this

[38] *Theocritus, Bion and Moschus,* by A. Lang, 1924, p. xviii.

[39] *Idyll,* II. 38 f. (Hallard).

[40] Edmond's rendering. Theocritus does not, like Thomas Hardy, emphasize the contrast between the beauty and the cruelty of nature, though he makes us recognize it. On Hardy, see Samuel C. Chew, *Thomas Hardy,* Bryn Mawr Notes and Monographs, III, 1921.

scene a striking statement made by Lindbergh in the first account he gave to the world of his famous crossing of the Atlantic? "I was glad," he wrote, "when the moon came up above the clouds. . . She was already past the full, but bright and comforting."[41] How near to the heart of a people this poem of Theocritus comes is shown by a ballad of love cited by Lang from the songs of modern Greece,[42] in which the same situation is found, and a similar appeal is made to the "bright, golden Moon." The *Phèdre* of Racine and the *Sister Helen* of Rossetti have both found inspiration in this wonderful idyll.

Thus, even in the idylls of city life, we find the poet is in close touch with nature. Cynisca's tears are "big as apples," and when her lover, angry at her leaning toward Master Wolf, struck her, off she rushed, as "in the old story the bull ran through the wood." And "as the swallow flies swiftly back to gather a morsel, fresh food, for her young ones under the eaves, still swifter sped she."[43] In the famous Fifteenth Idyll, a stupid man of the city can not tell the difference between sheep-

[41] San Francisco *Chronicle,* May 29, 1927.
[42] Lang, *Theocritus,* etc., p. xvii.
[43] Theocritus, *Idyll,* XIV (Lang).

fleeces and dogskins; Praxinoe, his wife, has a horror of horses and snakes; and people in the crowd jostle one another like a herd of swine. Among the decorations of the Adonis figure

> "*little Loves are fluttering*
> *Like new-fledged nightingales flitting from spray to spray on the wing,*"[44]

and in the morning the women are to "gather with the dew, and carry him forth among the waves that break upon the beach." Surely to this group on the sea-sands in the early hours of the dawn, the charms of nature bring no little joy as "with locks unloosed, and ungirt raiment falling to the ankles, and bosoms bare" these devotees begin their "shrill sweet song."[45]

But it is in his country idylls or pastorals proper that we find the real Theocritean delight in nature. Emerson begins his *Wood Notes* thus:

> "*When the pine tosses its cones*
> *To the song of its waterfall tones,*"

and Theocritus opens with the words:

[44] *Idyll,* XV. 120 f. (Hallard).
[45] *Ibid.* 133 ff. (Lang).

"*Sweet is the music of yon whispering pine*
Beside the springs; and sweetly pipest thou,
Goatherd,"

but

"*Sweeter thy singing, shepherd, is to me*
Than the resounding murmur of the lynn
Which pours from yonder crag." [46]

Thus the music of wind and water is heard at the outset and if the shepherds and goatherds of Theocritus sing sweetly, it is because they are matched with Nature herself, and can

"*murmur near the running brooks*
A music sweeter than their own" [47]

The poet's swains sing beneath pines and oaks, elms and wild olives; near running waters and springs where the nymphs are known to dwell; by the shore

"*where the ripples*
Break with a gentle plash," [48]

and a Daphnis can see Galatea rise from the salt-water; or perhaps on a hillside fronting the dawn, or in the shade of lofty rocks, while

46 *Idyll,* I. 1 ff. (Hallard).
47 Wordsworth, *A Poet's Epitaph.*
48 *Idyll,* VI. 11 f. (Hallard).

"far below shines and murmurs the Sicilian sea."[49] And all the while the birds are warbling, the locusts are chattering, or the bees are humming. So

> "*Of songs be my house the home always,*
> *For neither sleep, nor a sudden spring-day,*
> *Nor flowers to the bees, are as sweet as they;*
> *I love the Muse and her song.*"[50]

Here, as later to Bion, spring is "thrice delightful,"[51] and the spring-day is sudden, because, as Lang reminds us, "spring in the south comes 'at one stride,'" then passes imperceptibly into summer and summer again into autumn. Thus the three periods are closely knit, and in the southern regions of Europe the year has normally but two seasons, winter and summer. The former, of course, brings its own pleasures, but it is the summer that is especially dear to Theocritus. "In summer it is sweet to lie beneath the sky by running water," and in the fruit-time the poet and his friends in Cos actually masquerade as goatherds and join the merry country-folk

[49] Lang, *Theocritus,* p. 46.
[50] *Idyll,* IX. 33 ff. (J. M. Edmonds' transl., in *The Loeb Classical Library,* 1912).
[51] Bion, III. 15.

in the feast of harvest-home. They first meet in the hour of noonday heat, when

> "*Asleep the lizard on the wall doth lie,*
> *Afield the crested larks no longer fly.*" [52]

Then, after a friendly singing match, they pass on to the orchard, where they recline on deep beds of fragrant reeds and fresh-cut leaves of vine.

> "*Arching overhead*
> *Thick boughs of elms and poplar-trees were spread,*
> *Hard by from out the Nymphs' own cave did fall*
> *The sacred stream with murmur musical.*
> *On shadowed boughs the burnt cicalas plied*
> *Their noisy task; deep in the thornbrake cried*
> *A little owl; doves moaned, and larks did sing,*
> *And banded bees flew buzzing round the spring.*
> *All breathed the scent the harvest season beats;*
> *Beneath us, round us, apples rolled, and pears,*
> *And wild-plums weighed the slender branches low;*
> *And wine-jars lost the seals of years ago.*" [53]

And then they plant the great fan on Demeter's corn-heap

> "*While she near by*
> *With smile divine upon her face doth stand*
> *Holding the sheaves and poppies in her hand.*" [54]

[52] *Idyll,* VII. 22 f. (Marion Miller, Boston, 1900).
[53] *Ibid.* 130–147 (Miller).
[54] *Ibid.* 156 f. (Miller).

For such a scene in modern poetry we find our closest parallels in the *Poems of Rural Life*, written in the Dorset dialect by William Barnes, who as a northern poet has a wider range of seasons than Theocritus, but shows the same spirit in the happy time of fruit-gathering; Barnes singing of

"*The happy zight, — the merry night,*
The men's delight, — The Harvest Hwome." [55]

Take too an afternoon scene, when the rustics are gathering in the hay, and Jean carries ale, bread, and cheese around for the workers,

"*An' there, vor fun, we dress'd her head*
Wi' nodden poppies bright an' red,
As we were catchen vrom our laps,
Below a woak, over bits an' draps,
A-haulen o' the corn." [56]

Jean is more human than Demeter, who is doubtless represented by a rude statue, though one daring translator, forgetting the Greek atmosphere of the original, supposes that here

[55] The refrain in "A Zong ov Harvest Hwome."

[56] From "A-haulen O' the Corn." Note what Professor Palgrave said of Barnes: "He has a truth united always to beauty in his drawing of character and of country ways — a pure love of nature, such as one sees in the best Greek or Roman writers, exalted and rendered more tender by his devout Christian spirit." (*The Life of William Barnes*, London, 1887, p. 313.)

"Theocritus may refer to a charming mortal present at the harvest-home." [57]

This passage, however, does suggest the rich humor of Theocritus, which is by no means limited to the scenes from city life, of which the Fifteenth Idyll is such a notable example. Thus Polyphemus longs to be a fish:

"O, *why at birth were gills and fins not mine?*
To *kiss thy hand I'd leapt into the brine,*
(T*hy mouth perchance denied*) *and brought with me*
Red *poppy-flowers, or snowdrops white for thee* —
T*hese bloom in Spring-time, those in Summer weather;*
So *ne'er could I have offered both together:*" [58]

and the goatherd of the Third Idyll, drawing near to the cavern of Amaryllis, cries: "Ah, would I were that humming-bee, and to thy cave might come dipping beneath the fern that hides thee, and the ivy leaves!" [59] When Battus, the herdsman, runs a thorn into his foot, he exclaims,[60] "How tiny is the wound, and how big a man it masters!" Even Pan,

[57] M. M. Miller, *The Greek Idylls,* p. 101, note 25.
[58] *Idyll,* XI. 54 ff. (Hallard).
[59] *Idyll,* III. 12 ff. (Lang).
[60] *Idyll,* IV. 56.

if he does not assist the lover, is to be flogged by the boys of Arcady, and driven, in summer-time, to the remote Aethiopians, and in mid-winter to the Edonians of the far North. To cap this pleasantry, the ideal life is the frog's: "Lads, the frog has a jolly life, he is not cumbered about a butler to his drink, for he has liquor by him unstinted." [61]

In marked distinction from this lightsome mood Theocritus, not infrequently, depicts nature — in her various forms — as showing sympathy for suffering mortals. Thus the singing goatherd Comatas was saved from death by the blunt-faced bees, which, when a cruel master had shut him up in a cedar chest, brought him from the meadows the "food of tender flowers." [62] But it is mainly because of Daphnis, the ideal herdsman, that nature is out of joint, and Tityrus

"*Shall sing how Daphnis of old for Xenea came to die,*
And how the hills complained, and the oaks made moan that day
On Himeras' river-banks as the boy's life waned away

[61] *Idyll,* X. 52 ff. (Lang).
[62] *Idyll,* VII. 78 ff. Cf. Wordsworth's *Prelude,* Book XI, *fin.*

Like snow that melts in the glens of Haemus or Rhodope,
Or Athos, or where the slopes of utmost Caucasus be." [63]

The main theme of the First Idyll, most famous of the poems of Theocritus, is this "Death of Daphnis." In this poem Thyrsis, a shepherd of Aetna cries:

"*Where were ye, Nymphs, oh, where, when Daphnis pined away?*
Not where Anapus flows, or the waters of Acis are springing;
Not on Aetna's peak, but on Pindus, or Tempe's knolls that day," [64]

lines which Milton repeats so beautifully in his

"*Where were ye, Nymphs, when the remorseless deep*
Closed o'er the head of your loved Lycidas?"

The creatures of the wild, jackals, wolves, and lions, and of course the kine and bulls, heifers and calves, all mourned for him and to these in his last moments he made farewell, as also to the springs and streams of his native land:

[63] *Idyll,* VII. 72 ff. (Hallard).
[64] *Idyll,* I. 66 ff. (Hallard).

"*Ye wolves and jackals of the wild, bears of the mountain den,*
Farewell, for never shall ye see the herdsman Daphnis more,
No more in field or forest glade, in woodland ne'er again.
Farewell, O Arethusa! Good-night, ye streams that pour
Your waters bright and beautiful adown through Thymbris' glen!" [65]

Here surely Theocritus is in close touch with Sophocles,[66] with whose Ajax and Philoctetes Daphnis is in such striking accord. Bion and Moschus take up the same strain, the former in his *Woe, woe for Adonis*,[67] and the latter in his *Lament for Bion*.[68] Virgil repeats the theme in his Tenth Eclogue, as he sorrows with Gallus, and in modern poetry it reappears again and again, as in Milton's *Lycidas*, Pope's *Pastorals*, especially *Autumn* and *Winter*, Shelley's *Adonais*, and Matthew Arnold's *Thyrsis*. As to recent poets, Nathan Haskell Dole assures us that "the Idylls of Theocritus and their feebler echoes in Bion and Moschus have had

[65] *Idyll*, I. 115 ff. (Miller).
[66] See pp. 130 ff. above.
[67] Bion, I.
[68] Moschus, III.

a more powerful influence on modern poetry than any others of the works of the Greek poets." [69]

The feeling for nature which we have now traced from Homer to Theocritus might easily be followed up in still later Greek poets, but our space will not allow us to do more than call attention to one or two representatives of the *Palatine Anthology.*

This famous collection of short poems by various authors, known and unknown, ranging in date from the seventh century B.C. to the twelfth century A.D., has had a wide vogue in recent years. In England, many of the younger poets, like Richard Aldington, have been fascinated by its varied charms, and in America, Edwin Arlington Robinson takes from it his *Variations of Greek Themes,* while "H.D." in her preface to *Heliodora and Other Poems* acknowledges her obvious indebtedness.

One of the foremost women-poets of Greece, Anyte of Tegea, who belongs to the third century B.C., shows a very pretty fancy, when she makes the shining sea tremble, as it gazes on the bright image of Aphrodite in her shrine

[69] Cited by Kerlin, in *Theocritus in English Literature,* p. 163.

upon the shore.[70] These graceful verses too are given to a statue of Hermes: [71]

"*Here by the windswept orchard,*
Here where the three roads meet,
I watch the grey cliffs rising
And wayworn travellers greet.
My fountain murmurs cool and clear
Draw near and rest, O weary feet, draw near."

But the most captivating of these later writers is the Graeco-Syrian Meleager, whose home was in Gadara near the lake of Tiberias, and who flourished in the first century B.C. He indited verses to bees and gnats, crickets and grasshoppers, and gathered a "Garland," as he called it, of some forty poets, each of whom he associates with his favorite flower. Another wreath he is to make for his loved Heliodora:

"*White violet with the tender-leaved narcissus I will twine,*
And the laughing lips of lilies with myrtle blooms combine;
And I will bind the hyacinth, the dark red-purple flower,

[70] *Palatine Anthology*, IX. 144.
[71] *Ibid.* IX. 314 (tr. by F. A. Wright, in *The Broadway Translations*, London and New York, n.d.)

With crocus sweet and roses that are the lovers' dower,
To make the wreath that Heliodore's curl-scented brow shall wear,
To strew with falling petals the glory of her hair." [72]

But far the most beautiful and characteristic of Meleager's poems is his "Song of Spring," which is "full of the freshness of youth" and has a lyrical quality that seems remarkably modern:

"*Bright spring time smiles with flowery sheen,*
Foul winter's winds have flown,
Dark earth is clothed in herbage green,
The leaves, her fresh made gown.
The meadows laugh and drink the dew,
Each morn is bright with roses new.

Now goatherds flute upon the lea,
And with their younglings play;
Unharmed the ships sail on the sea
As zephyrs give them way.
With ivy leaves their hair men twine,
And sing the god who gave the vine.

The ox-born bees pursue their toil,
While with the wax they strive,

[72] *Ibid.* V. 147 (Sir Rennell Rodd). This version is in *Love, Worship and Death,* London, 1919.

And labouring shape the golden spoil
In myriad chambered hive.
The swan his winter fastness leaves,
The swallow darts among the eaves.

Now woolly sheep together throng
And in their lambs rejoice;
The wine god leads the dance and song,
Earth opens at spring's voice.
The halcyons skim the waves above,
And nightingales fill all the grove.

When trees with tender leaves are gay,
And sailors sail the seas;
When shepherds pipe a roundelay,
And swarm the clustering bees;
When every bird is on the wing,
Then how can poets help but sing?" [73]

Tennyson sings,[74]

"*Now fades the last long streak of snow,*"
"*Now rings the woodland loud and long,*"

then adds,

"*and in my breast*
Spring wakens too."

[73] *Palatine Anthology*, IX. 363. The translation is by F. A. Wright, in his *The Poets of the Greek Anthology*, pp. 126 f.
[74] *In Memoriam.*

The thought in the Greek poet is similar, but wholly joyous, and free from that regret which

> "*Becomes an April violet,*"

for Meleager is in the mood of Walt Whitman,[75] who loves

> "*to sing with the birds*
> A *warble for joy of Lilac-time,*"

and for both Meleager and Whitman,

> "*Spring has risen with a laugh, a wild-rose in her mouth,*
> *And is singing, singing, singing thro' the world.*" [76]

[75] *Warble for Lilac-Time.*
[76] Fiona Macleod, *The Bells of Youth.*

IX. ROMAN LITERATURE

Is this thy vengeance, holy Venus, thine
. . . .
Forgetful how my rich prooemion makes
Thy glory fly along the Italian field,
In lays that will outlast thy Deity? [1] TENNYSON

Row us out from Desenzano, to your Sirmione row!
So they row'd, and there we landed — " O venusta Sirmio! "
There to me thro' all the groves of olive in the summer glow,
There beneath the Roman ruin where the purple flowers grow,
Came that " Ave atque Vale " of the Poet's hopeless woe,
Tenderest of Roman poets nineteen-hundred years ago.[2]
TENNYSON

Landscape-lover, lord of language,
more than he that sang the Works and Days,
All the chosen coin of fancy
flashing out from many a golden phrase;

Thou that singest wheat and woodland,
tilth and vineyard, hive and horse and herd;
All the charm of all the Muses
often flowering in a lonely word.[3] TENNYSON

The cold Licenza through the valley brawls;
Unchanged the forest rustles on the hill;
The plowman to his lagging oxen calls
Amid the self-same vines; and murmuring still
Adown the hollow rock the fountain falls
To yield the wandering herd its welcome chill.

[1] *Lucretius.*
[2] *" Frater Ave Atque Vale."*
[3] *To Virgil.*

Each sound to him so long familiar grown
Even now the poet's loving ear had known,
Could he but stand again within these walls
Which once the kindly gods made all his own.[4]

GEORGE MEASON WHICHER

ROMAN literature and Roman art are so intimately associated with Greece that they have almost as much right to be treated as phases of Greek culture as have the art and literature of Egyptian Alexandria. Roman literature, in fact, is largely a late chapter in the history of Greek thought, for so completely were Greek letters, philosophy, and religion taken over by the Romans into their life, that these formed not merely the foundation, but to an enormous extent also the walls and even the furniture of the cultural building which the Romans succeeded in erecting. So too with Roman art. Artistic processes were learned from Greece, Greek artists were freely employed, and much of the surviving art of Rome is Greek in both subject and conception.

This does not imply, however, that we are to deny to Roman literature and Roman art all originality. Far from it. Purely Roman

[4] "The House of Horace," in *Roman Pearls and Other Verses,* Amherst, 1926.

ideals and Roman characteristics find ample expression in the various forms of art, while Roman literature, notwithstanding the prominence of its Hellenic elements, proves to be "the living heir, not the lifeless reproduction of the genius of Greece." [5]

In expressing, therefore, their attitude toward nature, we may expect to find in the Roman writers much of the language and imagery of their Greek models. Indeed, Greek and Roman ideas will be found inextricably blended. In Horace, Faunus (or Pan) passes swiftly from his Arcadian Lycaeus to the Sabine Lucretilis; [6] in Virgil, both Pales and Apollo quit the fields [7] when the herdsman Daphnis dies, while on joyous occasions the Fauns, "ever-present gods" of the Italian rustics, dance merrily with the Greek Dryad maids.[8]

And yet, with all this assimilation of Greek religious and mythological ideas, the Roman writers disclose a native warmth of feeling that seems to give fresh life and vigor to conventional and seemingly out-worn modes of

[5] Sellar, *The Roman Poets of the Republic*, p. 5.
[6] Horace, *Carmina*, I. 17.
[7] Virgil, *Eclogues*, V. 35.
[8] Virgil, *Georgics*, I. 10 f.

thought, and one must be a very unsympathetic reader who fails to recognize in the literature of Rome a fresh outburst of the emotional life and spirit of mankind.

Ennius, the father of Roman literature, is himself a good illustration of the composite character of Roman intellectuality. He is called by Suetonius a "semi-Graecus," and he used to claim that he had three hearts, because he spoke Greek, Oscan, and Latin. And yet Ennius, who "first brought down from lovely Helicon a garland of evergreen leafage to win name and fame through the nations of Italy,"[9] served as a centurion in the Roman army, and became truly representative of Roman national spirit. The reverence paid to him by later generations is well expressed by Quintilian, when he says: "Let us worship Ennius like groves hallowed by age in which the great old oaks are not so much beautiful as awe-inspiring."[10]

Besides his great epic, the *Annales,* in eighteen books, Ennius wrote comedies, tragedies, and miscellaneous works, but of all this output there remain only scattered fragments from which we can gather a quite imperfect

[9] Lucretius, I. 117 ff. [10] Quintilian, X. 1.88.

knowledge of his worth. His influence, however, upon later writers was immense, and some of Virgil's most picturesque and impressive descriptions owe not a little color to the old master. Even in the extant remains we catch some glimpses of great beauty. Ennius loves the *silva frondosa,* "leafy forest," the *amoena salicta,* "sweet willow-groves," and the *ponti caerula prata,* "blue sea-meadows." He gives us a charming picture of a moonlight night,

lumine sic tremulo
terra et cava caerula candent,

"*thus with quivering light*
The earth and heaven's blue depths are bright,"[11]

and, to quote Duff, "his flash of golden sunrise with its effective close on a monosyllable —*simul aureus exoritur sol*— is as good as Coleridge's tropical sunset:

"*The sun's rim dips; the stars rush out:*
At one stride comes the dark."[12]

The writers intervening between Ennius and Lucretius need detain us but a moment. They

[11] From the *Melanippa,* as given by Lucian Mueller, *Q. Enni Carminum Reliquiae,* Fabulae, 363 f.
[12] J. Wight Duff, *A Literary History of Rome,* p. 150.

are chiefly the dramatists, Pacuvius and Accius in tragedy, Plautus and Terence in comedy. Ancient comedy, apart from Aristophanes, is not a field in which to expect a poetical appreciation of nature, and the only Roman comedy which might illustrate our subject is the *Rudens* of Plautus, an adaptation of some lost play by Diphilus, which "has all the charm and freshness of a sea-idyll."[13] The prologue is spoken by a star-god Aucturus, and the wild scenery of a lonely coast, combined with a romantic plot, has reminded its readers of *The Tempest* and *Pericles, Prince of Tyre.* This atmosphere, of course, may be wholly due to the Greek original.

The tragedians survive only in fragments, which again represent plays founded upon Greek subjects. Pacuvius, nephew of Ennius, was interested in natural philosophy, and one of his best known passages,[14] describing the *Aether* of the heavens, anticipates the scientific manner of Lucretius, while a second, rescued for us from the *Teucer* by Cicero, is a vivid description of a storm at sea.[15] Accius, who

[13] Sellar, *Roman Poets of the Republic,* p. 185.
[14] Cited and translated by Sellar, p. 137.
[15] Cited and translated by Sellar, p. 141; also, in verse, by Duff, pp. 226 f.

was born half a century later than Pacuvius, shows increasing imaginative power, and Sellar [16] quotes the following passage from the *Oenomaus* as "perhaps the first instance of Latin poetry of a descriptive passage which gives any hint of the pleasure derived from contemplating the common aspects of Nature":

> "*Mayhap ere Dawn, that heralds blazing beams,*
> *When yokels drive the new-waked ox afield,*
> *To cleave with plough the red dew-sprinkled soil,*
> *And from the yielding tilth to turn the clods.*" [17]

If thus far we have found in the Roman poets comparatively little evidence of an appreciation of nature, the defect is fully atoned for by the next important poet who is to be considered. Indeed, nowhere else, perhaps, in the world's literature can one point to a great writer who more richly exemplifies our theme than Lucretius.

In the *De Rerum Natura* the author deals from first to last with Nature herself. He breaks down the bars of her doors,[18] penetrates into her secret hiding-places,[19] and brings to

[16] Sellar, pp. 149 f.
[17] Translated by Duff, p. 230.
[18] *Effringere portarum claustra,* I. 70 f.
[19] *Caecasque latebras Insinuare omnis,* I. 408 f.

light the very laws which she herself has ordained and also obeys. Lucretius has solved once for all the question whether the same man can be both a scientist and a poet, for his splendid work is both a great poem and an exposition of a scientific system.[20] To be sure, a modern writer would naturally present scientific material in prose, but the Democritean theory of the physical world which Epicurus accepted and Lucretius sets forth is more than cold science. It is an apocalypse, a revelation, which is proclaimed with almost fanatical zeal, and with a spiritual exaltation that lifts it far above the common level of intellectual thought. For Epicurus, who

> "*fared afar, beyond*
> *The flaming ramparts of the world,*"[21]

is the Saviour, who will free mankind from a terrible curse, the fear of the gods and the fear of death, and his gospel is therefore

[20] Cf. W. H. Mallock, in his Preface to *Lucretius on Life and Death,* p. vi: "Lucretius was, so far as the knowledge of his time would allow him to be, as completely and as consciously a scientific man and a physicist as Darwin, or Huxley, or any of our contemporary evolutionists."

[21] I. 72 (William Ellery Leonard's translation, London and New York, 1916).

preached with all the fiery earnestness of an enthusiastic convert to a new faith.

Thus Lucretius deals with the universe itself and with cosmic forces. He is concerned with the ultimate elements, with the indestructibility of matter, with the conservation of energy, with the infinity of space and with the process of world-building — in a word, with a nature which is the product of purely physical forces and has no dependence upon personal or supernatural beings, for as Mrs. Browning puts it,

> *" he denied*
> D*ivinely the divine,"* [22]

and saw in mere Matter " the promise and potency of every form and quality of life.[23] But if Lucretius, who has been able to cast off " the terror and darkness of mind " [24] by which his fellow-men were oppressed, has also cast off all belief in creative deity and a world built by design, he has not thereby lost the reverence and adoration which most men instinctively

[22] From *A Vision of Poets.*

[23] From John Tyndall's address as President of the British Association, 1874.

[24] Lucretius, II. 146.

pay to the Divine Energy through whom "we live and move and have our being." Nature herself becomes God to Lucretius. She is the *creatrix*,[25] the "cunning fashioner of things," *natura daedala rerum*,[26] who controls all life and to whose accents man may listen, when disposed to lament his lot.[27] She is, in fact, herself divine, and under the guise of an adorable goddess appears in that most beautiful invocation which this greatest of rationalist poets addresses to "the Mother of the Roman race, benign Venus."[28]

But in our rapid survey we cannot discuss the science, philosophy, or theology of Lucretius, though all such subjects are involved in any adequate treatment of the poet's appreciation of nature. Let it suffice to note briefly some of the innumerable passages in the poem which make a powerful appeal to the modern nature-lover, for like his own *alma Venus*, Lucretius also journeys "amid seas and mountains and sweeping rivers and leafy homes of birds and verdant plains."[29]

[25] *Ibid.* II. 1117.
[26] *Ibid.* V. 234.
[27] *Ibid.* III. 931 ff.
[28] *Ibid.* I. 1 ff. See Chapter II, above.
[29] *Ibid.* I. 17 f.

As to the sea, Lucretius loves the prospect from the land, *suave mari magno*, for,

> "*When storms blow loud, 'tis sweet to watch at ease*
> *From shore, the sailor laboring with the seas.*"[30]

and he warns us to "eschew the treacherous deep . . . and never trust her at any time when the calm sea shows her false alluring smile."[31] He has seen at times a black cloud, like a flood of pitch

> "*down on the waves*
> *Fall with vast uproar*"

so that

> "*Back on the lands the people shudder round*
> *And seek for cover.*"[32]

And again he notes how varied shells may paint the lap of earth

> "*Where, with soft waves, the sea*
> *Beats on the thirsty sands of curving shores.*"[33]

or how

> "*What was black of hue an hour ago*
> *Can of a sudden like the marble gleam,—*

[30] II. 1 f. (W. H. Mallock).
[31] II. 557 ff. (W. H. D. Rouse, in *The Loeb Classical Library*, 1924).
[32] VI. 256 ff. (Leonard).
[33] II. 374 ff. (Leonard).

As ocean, when the high winds have upheaved
Its level plains, is changed to hoary waves
Of marble whiteness." [34]

Of distant seas, Lucretius may have had personal knowledge of the Black Sea, or Pontus,

" *That sea which floweth forth with fixèd tides,*
Keeping one onward tenor as it glides," [35]

a passage which, indirectly, and perhaps transmitted through the elder Seneca, has left its impress on Shakespeare:

" *like to the Pontick Sea,*
Whose icy current and compulsive course
Ne'er feels retiring flood, but keeps due on
To the Propontick and the Hellespont." [36]

As to mountains, Lucretius had himself climbed them, and from their summits observed the movements of the clouds.[37] He knows that on great mountains fire will sometimes break out, when the topmost branches of tall trees are rubbed together by the wind.[38] To prove that atoms may be in motion though seemingly at rest, Lucretius vividly describes

[34] II. 764 ff. (Leonard).
[35] V. 507 f. (Leonard).
[36] *Othello,* III. 3, cf. Seneca, *Nat. Q.,* IV. 2.29.
[37] VI. 451–469.
[38] I. 897 ff.

the mimicry of war, when soldiers are marching and countermarching on the plains, the cavalry galloping hither and thither, and the bronze weapons gleaming, and yet to one looking on from some mountain height, they all seem to stand still, a spot of brightness resting on the levels below.[39] Moreover, the poet has heard the hills repeat echoes six or seven times, when on shady mountains he and others have shouted to their straying comrades:

> "*And these spots*
> *The neighbouring country-side doth feign to be*
> *Haunts of the goat-foot satyrs and the nymphs;*
> *And tells ye there be fauns, by whose night noise*
> *And antic revels yonder they declare*
> *The voiceless silences are broken oft,*
> *And tones of strings are made and wailings sweet*
> *Which the pipe, beat by players' finger-tips,*
> *Pours out; and far and wide the farmer-race*
> *Begins to hear, when, shaking the garmentings*
> *Of pine upon his half-beast head, god-Pan*
> *With puckered lips oft runneth o'er and o'er*
> *The open reeds, — lest flute should cease to pour*
> *The woodland music!*"[40]

The beautifully idyllic spirit here illustrated is paralleled in another imaginative passage where

[39] II. 323 ff.
[40] IV. 572 ff. (Leonard for 580–589).

in sketching the primitive life of man Lucretius explains the origin of music, vocal and instrumental:

> "*But by the mouth*
> *To imitate the liquid notes of birds*
> *Was earlier far 'mongst men than power to make,*
> *By measured song, melodious verse and give*
> *Delight to ears. And whistlings of the wind*
> *Athrough the hollows of the reeds first taught*
> *The peasantry to blow into the stalks*
> *Of hollow hemlock-herb. Then bit by bit*
> *They learned sweet plainings, such as pipe outpours,*
> *Beaten by finger-tips of singing men,*
> *When heard through unpathed groves and forest deeps*
> *And woodsy meadows, through the untrod haunts*
> *Of shepherd folk and spots divinely still.*" [41]

Surely the poet who could thus dwell upon the *avia nemora,* the *silvæ saltusque,* and the *loca deserta* must have loved the forests and mountains, and often sought the *otia dia,* which, perhaps, he could find there only. And surely it was in such haunts that he drew near to the heart of Nature, the only divinity he wor-

41 V. 1379–1389 (Leonard).

shipped,[42] meditating his muse and building his lofty rhyme, for, to let him tell his own story,

> "I *wander afield, thriving in sturdy thought,*
> T*hrough unpathed haunts of the Pierides,*
> T*rodden by step of none before. I joy*
> T*o come on undefilèd fountains there,*
> T*o drain them deep; I joy to pluck new flowers,*
> T*o seek for this my head a signal crown*
> F*rom regions where the Muses never yet*
> H*ave garlanded the temples of a man.*" [43]

True Italian as he is, Lucretius knows the ways of rivers. He has watched them at the source;[44] he has seen them rushing down from the great mountains;[45] he is familiar with them as they flow level with their banks, which they are slowly eating away,[46] as well as in flood-time, "when a great deluge of water from the high mountains swells the flood with torrents of rain, dashing together wreckage of forests and whole trees, nor can strong bridges withstand the sudden force of the coming water." [47] Of foreign rivers, the Nile is of unusual interest,

[42] See, however, "Lucretius as a Student of Roman Religion," in *T.A.P.A.* 145–160 (1918).
[43] I. 925–930 (Leonard).
[44] V. 270.
[45] V. 946.
[46] II. 362, and V. 256.
[47] I. 282 ff. (Rouse).

and Lucretius speculates at length upon the extraordinary phenomenon of its rising:[48]

> " P*erchance, his waters wax, O far away,*
> A*mong the Aethiopians' lofty mountains*
> W*hen the all-beholding sun with thawing beams*
> D*rives the white snows to flow into the vales.*" [49]

But it is not merely a mighty flood that appeals to Lucretius; all running water has peculiar charms for him, as may be seen from this delightful picture of early man: " As they roamed abroad they dwelt in familiar woodland precincts of the Nymphs, whence they knew that some running rivulet issued rippling over the wet rocks, rippling over the rocks in abundant flow and dripping upon the green moss, with plenty left to splash and bubble over the level plain." [50]

Such lovely scenes even the rationalist poet can portray as the abode of Nymphs, and it is not surprising to find that " amid all his speculation he retained his love of the simple beauty of the lowliest flower, and his interest in the welfare of every living creature.[51] He marshals before us " the race of men, and the dumb swimming tribes of scaly fish, happy cattle, and wild

[48] VI. 712 ff.
[49] VI. 735 ff. (Leonard).
[50] V. 948 ff. (Rouse).
[51] Geikie, p. 56.

beasts, the many kinds of birds which throng the joyous regions of water around bank and spring and lake, crowding the pathless woods through and through as they flit about." [52] For the birds he seems to have had peculiar affection, and delights to see them,

> "*Flit round the trackless forests, with liquid notes*
> *Filling the regions along the mellow air,*" [53]

while among the domestic animals he is especially fond of the dog.[54] At the same time his sympathy for the cow that has been robbed of her calf is among the famous passages in ancient literature, and can be duplicated only in Virgil.[55]

Yet it is the larger aspects of nature that are most conspicuous in Lucretius. He gives us vivid pictures of the wonders of the heavens, the clouds, the stormy seas, ruinous earthquakes, and volcanic eruptions, but he is also a cosmic poet, and sings of world-creative forces. Further, in imaginative insight, says Mackail, "he is unsurpassed, if not unequalled." No one, at least no poet, has given a more realistic sketch of the infancy of the world. "Before his imagination the earth rises

[52] II. 342 ff. (Rouse).
[53] II. 145 f. (Leonard).
[54] Geikie, pp. 182 ff.
[55] II. 352 ff.

swathed in tropical forests, and all strange forms of life issuing and jostling one another for existence in the steaming warmth of perpetual summer. Among a thousand types that flowered and fell, the feeble form of primitive man is distinguished without fire, without clothing, without articulate speech." [56] No wonder that such a poet " goes straight to the mind of the scientific inquirer of today and any age." [57] His scientific imagination appealed strongly to Tyndall, and his unique qualities so captivated Tennyson that they inspired one of the laureate's most remarkable poems, the *Lucretius*.

Catullus, a young contemporary of Lucretius, is famous as the most spontaneous lyric poet of Rome, and is classed by some enthusiastic admirers with Sappho and Shelley. Singing as he does of love, of course he also sings of springtime,

Iam ver egelidos refert tepores [58]

" *Warm spring is here: the cold is gone,*"

and of other beautiful things, such as his home in that most picturesque region, the lake coun-

[56] J. W. Mackail, *Latin Literature,* New York, 1895, p. 45.

[57] Duff, *A Literary History of Rome,* p. 302.

[58] *Catullus,* XLVI. with F. A. Wright's rendering, London and New York, 1906.

try of northern Italy, where, nineteen hundred years later, the English laureate

> " *Wandered to and fro*
> *Gazing at the Lydian laughter of the Garda Lake below*
> *Sweet Catullus's all-but-island, olive-silvery Sirmio!* "[59]

It may well be that from his " all-but-island " home Catullus many a time saw such wondrous sunrises over the water as he has pictured so beautifully in his *Marriage of Peleus and Thetis:*

> " *Zephyrus, roughening with his morning breeze*
> *The placid sea, stirs from their sleep the waves,*
> *As 'neath the threshold of the wandering Sun*
> *The golden Dawn arises — and at first*
> *Slowly they heave, rocked by the gentle breeze,*
> *And lightly plash with lilting laughter's sound;*
> *But with the freshening wind, thicker they crowd,*
> *And gleam in the rosy light as they float away.*"[60]

Flowers, too, were dear to the poet's heart:

> " *Look how a flower in some close garden grows,*
> *Hid from rude cattle, bruised by no plows,*

[59] Tennyson, "*Frater Ave Atque Vale.*" Cf. *Catullus* XXXI and CI.

[60] *Catullus,* LXIV. 269 ff. (Rendering of Charles Ernest Bennett, in *Across the Years,* Boston, 1917, p. 14.)

Wind-stroked, sun-strengthened, nurtured by the
rain:
To pluck it, many a youth and maid is fain!
But once 'tis culled, its beauty fades away:
No youth, no maid desires it from that day." [61]

Junia, fair bride of Manlius, is like the garden's joy,[62] a lovely 'hyacinthus,' which is probably our iris or larkspur; or again she suggests

" *Some white marguerite*
Or poppy's yellow bloom." [63]

As is well known, Catullus was born in Cisalpine Gaul, and some scholars detect in him a Celtic strain, due to his environment, if not to blood. At any rate, he exhibits not merely a fiery, passionate, emotional nature, unparalleled among the Roman poets, but also something of that interest in the life of the wild that animates the *Bacchae* of Euripides. Hence his beautiful hymn to Diana, " goddess of the vast forest that lay above his home lake, a woodland goddess of the barbarous mountain tribes:[64]

[61] *Catullus,* LXII. 39 ff. (Wright).
[62] *Catullus,* LXI. 91 ff.
[63] *Ibid.* 194 f. (Duff).
[64] Tenney Frank, *Catullus and Horace,* New York, 1928, p. 9.

Montium domina ut fores
Silvarumque virentium
Saltuumque reconditorum
Amniumque sonantum

(" that thou mightest be the lady of mountains and green woods, and sequestered glens and sounding rivers").[65] It is from such a mountain that Chiron, the Centaur, brought his sylvan gifts, to lay at the feet of Thetis, the bride:

" *First of the gods, from Pelion's rugged height*
With sylvan gifts, Chiron the Centaur came.
For all the lovely flowers the meadows bear,
On Thessaly's towering mountain heights, and all
That warm Favonius with his kindly breath
Summons to life beside the running streams —
All these in sweet confusion did he bear." [66]

Such a mountain was Cytorus, where

Loquente saepe sibilum edidit coma [67]

" *Sweet whispering winds her leaves would thrill,"*

and it was down some familiar mountain-side that the poet saw leap the crystal water, with which he compares his own, the lover's, tears:

[65] *Catullus, English Translation,* Cambridge, England, 1904, XXXIV. 9 ff., with rendering by F. W. Cornish.
[66] *Catullus,* LXIV. 278 ff. (C. E. Bennett).
[67] *Ibid.* IV. 12 (R. Kennard Davis, London, 1913).

"*As some clear stream, from mossy stone that leaps,*
Far up among the hills, and, wimpling down
By wood and vale, its onward current keeps
To lonely hamlet and to stirring town,
Cheering the wayworn traveller as it flows
When all the fields with drought are parched and bare." [68]

Surely Sir Archibald Geikie might have excepted Catullus, when he declares that the Roman poets had no appreciation of mountain scenery.[69] Tenney Frank is inclined to think that in this striking picture we have "a reminiscence of one of the many capricious cascades high on the mountain-side that one passes in the Adige valley as one travels north from Verona to Trent." [70] He adds suggestively, "Had Catullus written fifty years later, after the mountain folk had been pacified so that the Alps were made accessible to Roman travellers, he might well have discovered mountain landscapes as a theme for poetry." It must be hard to appreciate the beauty of mountains when

[68] *Ibid.* LXVIII. 57 ff. (Martin).
[69] Geikie, *The Love of Nature Among the Romans*, p. 292.
[70] *Catullus and Horace*, p. 47.

you can not traverse them without imperilling your life.

As for the sea, all students of Catullus are familiar with the majestic opening of the sad elegy on his brother's death,

> Multas per gentes et multa per aequora vectus
>
> "*Through many a region borne, o'er many a main,*" [71]

as well as with the gay picture of the yacht, which in old age tells the story of her life:

> "*Stranger, the ship that here you see*
> *Swiftest of vessels claims to be,*
> *For she could make a beaten boat*
> *Of any racing craft afloat,*
> *Whether by rowing she'd prevail,*
> *Or scud beneath the snowy sail!*" [72]

The " large air " of the sea is also breathed in the *Marriage of Peleus and Thetis.* There the ship of pine from Pelion's summit breasted the clear waters, and as " she ploughed the windy expanse and the wave churned by the oars grew white with foam-flakes, forth looked from the foaming surge the Nereids of the deep,

[71] *Catullus,* CI. (R. Kennard Davis).
[72] *Ibid.* IV. (Davis).

wondering at the strange thing," [73] a scene strongly Euripidean in character.

Before leaving Catullus, we must glance at still another poem which is filled from first to last with the spirit of the wild. The *Attis*,[74] a marvellous *tour de force*, is unique in both Greek and Latin literature. It is a singularly dramatic story of a Greek youth, who consecrating himself to the service of Cybele, the Phrygian Magna Mater, makes himself a eunuch, and withdraws to the slopes of lonely Mount Ida, far from home and country and friends.

> "*Across the roaring ocean, with heart and with eye of flame,*
> *To the Phrygian forest Attis in an eager frenzy came:*
> *And he leapt from his lofty vessel, and he stood in the groves of pine*
> *That circled round with shadows Cybele's mystic shrine.*"

There, after performing the terrible initiatory rite, he leads his comrades up to the shrine of the goddess, where he and they fall asleep

[73] *Ibid.* LXIV. 1–15 (Cornish).

[74] *Catullus,* LXIII. (Grant Allen, *The Attis of Catullus,* London, 1892).

through exhaustion. Repentance comes with the morrow:

"*Shall I dwell on the icy ridges under Ida's chilly*
blast?
Shall I pass my days in the shadows that the
Phrygian summits cast,
With the stag that haunts the forest, with the
boar that roams the glade?
Even now my soul repents me: even now is my
fury stayed."

But the inexorable goddess claims the service due:

"*There all the days of his lifetime as Cybele's*
thrall he passed."

No one can convey in an English translation an adequate idea of the extraordinary character of the original verse, but Grant Allen, who sees in the *Attis* "the finest flower of the Celtic genius, infiltrated by the mystic and mysterious charm of the Oriental imagination," has at least appreciated its significance in the history of religious thought, and has also made a brave attempt to convey to English readers somthing of the lightness and swiftness of a metre that defies imitation.[75]

[75] Professor Tyrrell depreciates Grant Allen's laudable effort, but it is the best so far made. Leigh Hunt's given by Wright in his *Catullus* is as heavy as lead beside it.

Virgil, greatest of all the Roman poets, is full of love for nature. This is one of the chief charms of the *Eclogues*, it permeates the *Georgics,* and is a prominent characteristic of the *Aeneid.* The *Eclogues,* being largely imitative of Theocritus, reproduce much of the scenery and thought of the *Idylls,* but scenery in the *Eclogues* is not Sicilian alone and much of the imagery and sentiment is purely Virgilian. In the First and Ninth of these poems Virgil writes of his own farm in the Mantuan district, and Professor Conway has shown that, in spite of prevailing incredulity, even today we can identify almost certainly the precise locality which the poet describes, "where the hills begin to rise, then sink their ridge in a gentle slope, down to the water and the old beeches with their now shattered tops."[76]

This northern country between the Alps and the Po, where Virgil was born, was always close to the poet's heart. Some day he hoped to win palms of victory for his beloved Mantua, and set up to Augustus a temple "where great Mincius wanders in slow windings and fringes

[76] *Ecl.,* IX. 7 ff. Cf. R. S. Conway, *Harvard Lectures on the Vergilian Age,* Ch. 2.

his banks with slender reeds."[77] He glories in his native lakes:

anne lacus tantos? te, Lari maxime, teque
fluctibus et fremitu adsurgens Benace marino?[78]

(lines which long afterwards haunted the English Virgil, when he visited this beautiful region), and again as late as the Tenth *Aeneid*,[79] Virgil speaks with pride of Mantua, partly Tuscan in origin, side by side with the Mincius, "child of Benacus." A bitter lot it must have been for one to be driven from those "sweet fields,"[80] where "amid familiar streams and sacred springs," one might "court the cooling shade."[81] Here was the willow hedge with its gentle hum of bees; here, the towering rock, beneath which the woodman sang; here was the lofty elm, where cooing pigeons and turtledoves were ever moaning; and here, as evening twilight drew near, one might see "the lengthening shadows fall from mountain heights."[82]

The green alder shooting up in the early spring is a fitting symbol for Virgil's increasing

[77] *Georg.*, III. 12 ff.
[78] *Georg.*, II. 159 f. See p. 15 above.
[79] *Aen.*, X. 198 ff.
[80] *Ecl.*, I. 3.
[81] *Ecl.*, I. 51 f.
[82] *Ecl.*, I. 53 ff. and 83.

love for a dear friend;[83] a beautiful song is "like sleep on the grass to the weary, amid summer heat like the slaking of thirst in a dancing rill of sweet water,"[84] it has more charm than "the rustle of the rising South, the beach lashed by surge, and streams tumbling down amid rocky glens."[85] The song which wins so wonderful a tribute is a song of Caesar, "lover of peace," now exalted to the heavens. In his glorification all Nature rejoices, "frolic glee seizes the woods and all the countryside, and Pan, and the shepherds, and the Dryad maids."[86] This same Nature, when Gallus was pining away, was in deep distress: "even the laurels, even the tamarisks wept, yea, pine-crowned Maenalus, and the crags of cold Lycaeus."[87]

It is in the *Georgics,* however, that Virgil is most clearly revealed as a poet of nature. These polished poems are partly autobiographical, and we learn from them something of the poet's mental and spiritual life. In the Sixth

[83] *Ecl.,* x. 73 f.
[84] *Ecl.,* v. 45 ff.
[85] *Ecl.,* v. 82 ff.
[86] *Ecl.,* v. 58 ff.
[87] *Ecl.,* x. 13 ff. I take it that much of the sentiment of this poem is humorous. Virgil is rallying his friend on his love affair with Lycoris, an actress.

Eclogue[88] Virgil had Silenus sing a song of creation, which may be regarded as an epitome of the great poem of Lucretius, and in a remarkable passage in the Second *Georgic*[89] Virgil confesses that it was his own dearest ambition to have the Muses, whose priest he was, reveal to him the laws of Nature. "But if," as he fears, "the chill blood about the heart may bar him from reaching these realms," then, he cries, "let my delight be the country, and the running streams amid the dells — may I love the waters and the woods, though fame be lost. O for those plains, and Spercheus, and Taygetus, where Spartan girls hold Bacchic rites! O for one to set me in the cool glens of Haemus, and shield me under the branches' mighty shade!"

Here follows the famous contrast between the philosopher "who has been able to win knowledge of the causes of things, casting beneath his feet all fear and unyielding Fate, and the howls of hungry Acheron," and the simple man of the country, who in all innocence worships his rural gods. The former is *felix* — his lot is a *blessed* one; but the latter also is

[88] *Ecl.*, VI. 31 ff.

[89] *Georg.*, II. 475 ff. My own translation of *Virgil* in *The Loeb Classical Library*, 1922, is freely used.

fortunatus — he too is truly happy. If Virgil can not be a Lucretius, he will be content with the minor rôle, finding inspiration in the woods and waters of the country, the haunts of "Pan and old Silvanus and the sister Nymphs."

Virgil's delight in the waters and woods and indeed every aspect of the country is seen from first to last in the *Georgics*. "Quid faciat laetas segetes," "what makes the crops joyous?" is his very first utterance, and this note of joy, though not the only note, is heard in every book. The *Georgics,* in fact, are a eulogy, a rhapsody, almost, upon the farmer's life, and it is Virgil's genuine love of nature and country-life that has turned what might have been a mere didactic treatise into a poem full of warm sentiment and beauty.[90]

Virgil was as much a poet of the "Seasons" as was the English Thomson, but his descriptions are scattered through his work. And chiefly does he delight in summer and spring. In "joyous summer" he would have us "haste to the cool fields, as the morning star begins to rise, while the day is young, while the grass is hoar, and the dew on the tender blade most

[90] See Chapter IV above.

sweet to the cattle. Then, when heaven's fourth hour has brought thirst to all, and the plaintive cicalas rend the thickets with song, I will bid the flocks at the side of wells or deep pools drink of the water that runs in oaken channels. But in midday heat let them seek out a shady dell, where haply Jove's mighty oak with its ancient trunk stretches out giant branches, or where the grove, black with many holms, lies brooding with hallowed shade. Then give them once more the trickling stream, and once more feed them till sunset, when the cool evening star allays the air, and the moon, now dropping dew, gives strength to the glades, when the shores ring with the halcyon, and the copses with the finch."[91] But

> "*Spring, the sweet spring, is the year's pleasant king*"[92]

and Virgil, elated by the beauty and glory of this season in Italy, where you may find it at all times, *hic ver adsiduum,*[93] dreams that at such a lovely time the world itself was created, "when," as the Hebrew poet puts it, "the morning stars sang together, and all the sons

[91] *Georg.*, III. 322 ff.
[92] Thomas Nash.
[93] *Georg.*, II. 149.

of God shouted for joy!"[94] Then it is that "pathless copses ring with birds melodious, and in their settled time the herds renew their loves. The bountiful land brings forth, and beneath the West's warm breezes the fields loosen their bosoms; in all things abounds soft moisture, and the grasses safely dare to trust themselves to face the new suns; the vine-tendrils fear not the rising of the South, or a storm driven down the sky by mighty blasts of the North, but thrust forth their buds and unfold all their leaves. Even such days, I could suppose, shone at the first dawn of the infant world; even such was the course they held. Spring-time that was; the great world was keeping spring, and the East-winds spared their wintry blasts, when the first cattle drank in the light, and man's iron race reared its head from the hard fields, and wild beasts were let loose into the forests and the stars into heaven."[95] It is in this same book, the second, that Virgil bursts into his famous eulogy of Italy[96] — a land of corn and wine and oil, of flocks and herds and snowy bulls — a land where spring abides and summer lingers, a land free from

[94] *Job*, 38.7
[95] *Georg.*, II. 328 ff.
[96] *Georg.*, II. 136 ff.

savage beasts and noxious herbs. This land has noble cities on its hills, and rivers that flow beneath their ancient walls. It has seas and lakes, wondrous harbors and mines, but above all, men — hardy warriors and heroic leaders. No wonder that at this point the poet rises to salute the land of which he is so proud.

Salve, magna parens frugum, Saturnia tellus,
Magna virum!

"*Hail, land of Saturn, great mother of earth's fruits, great mother of men!*"

It is for such a land that he "essays his theme of olden praise and art."

Virgil's constant practice of personalizing Nature is one of the *Georgics'* most striking characteristics. His lands feel the sun and frost, they rest under a change of crop, and are not thankless if left unploughed. The fields commonly rejoice, but mourn when they lose their tillers. Soils have hereditary features, and may be churlish and unfriendly, yet "not mine be that over-fruitful soil, and may it not show itself too strong when the ears are young!" Mysia glories in her tillage, and Gargarus marvels at his harvests.[97]

[97] *Georg.*, I. 48, 71, 83, 101 ff., 507; II. 177 ff., 252.

Virgil's sympathy with the lower creatures is profound. "Bird, beast, and insect were scanned by his closely observant eyes, with all the sympathy of his gentle and kindly heart." [98] His picture of the steer that sorrows for his brother's death may be compared with that of Lucretius where the cow is robbed of her calf.[99] Animal life is also treated with delightful humor. The *improbus anser,* "rascally goose," may do some mischief, the mouse "sets up a home and builds storehouses," the toiling ant is "anxious for its destitute old age," the frogs "croak their old-time plaint," the sea-birds play with one another in the surf; the raven "in solitary state stalks along the dry sea-sand," and the owl "watching the sunset from some high peak, vainly plies her evening song." [100] As for bees, they are treated throughout a whole book as "a wondrous pageant of a tiny world, showing chiefs great-hearted, a whole nation's character and tastes and tribes and battles." [101]

The fruits and flowers, vegetables and trees

[98] Geikie, *The Love of Nature Among the Romans,* p. 187.

[99] *Georg.,* III. 515 ff., cf. p. 196 above.

[100] *Georg.,* I. 119, 181 f., 186, 378, 383 ff., 388, 402 f.

[101] *Georg.,* IV. 3 ff.

of gardens, were all dear to Virgil's heart. In one passage [102] he sketches what might have been a fifth *Georgic,* a book on gardens, in which he would have sung "of the rose-beds of twice-blooming Paestum; how the endive rejoices in the stream it drinks, and the green banks in the parsley; and how the gourd, winding along the ground, swells into its paunch. Nor had I been silent of the late-blooming narcissus, or the curling acanthus-stem, the pale ivy or the shore-loving myrtle." And then comes the charming picture of the old Corycian, once perhaps a pirate, but now turned gardener "under the towers of Oebalia's citadel," [103] who had made his few acres of poor soil blossom with white lilies, vervain, and slender poppy, and was happy as a king. He was the first to pluck roses and apples in season, his hyacinths flowered before winter was sped. Luxuriant were his limes and laurestines [104] — that graceful shrub which is among the first to burst into bloom in early spring, and therefore is planted by the wise bee-keeper. Elms and pears, black

[102] *Georg.,* IV. 116 ff.

[103] i.e. Tarentum, in southern Italy.

[104] That *tinus,* not *pinus,* should be read in *Georg.,* IV. 141, and *tinos,* not *pinos,* in *Georg.,* IV. 112, is maintained by the writer in an article on "The Tinus in Virgil," in *Classical Philology,* X. 405–410 (1915).

thorns and plane-trees — all these the old man could transplant when fully grown.

The most beautiful narrative in all Virgil is the story of Orpheus and Eurydice, taken, to be sure, from some unknown Greek source, but told with that inimitable art of which Virgil alone was capable.[105] The whole episode in which it occurs is a substitute for a passage which dealt with Egypt and its first governor under Rome, Virgil's dear friend Gallus, and it is quite possible that the marvellous pathos of the story we now read reflects the poet's grief over the sad and untimely end of Gallus, who, being suspected of disloyalty to Augustus, took his own life. Gladly would Virgil have brought his friend back from the grave, but even Orpheus could not

" quite set free
His half regain'd Eurydice."

Be that as it may, in supremely beautiful and moving verse Virgil tells of Orpheus' visit to the world of the dead.[106] "Startled by his

[105] I am sorry to read in H. W. Prescott's *The Development of Virgil's Art*, Chicago, 1927, p. 132, that "probably there is little Virgilian art and material in this narrative." There is doubtless little original material, but why deny to the poet the exquisite art?

[106] *Georg.*, IV. 464 ff.

strain, there came from the lowest realms of Erebus the bodiless shadows and the phantoms of those bereft of light, in multitude like the thousands of birds that hide amid the leaves when the evening star or a wintry shower drives them from the hills. . . Nay, the very halls of Hell were spell-bound, and inmost Tartarus, and the Furies with livid snakes entwined in their locks. Cerberus held agape his triple mouths, and Ixion's wheel was stayed by the still wind." And now Eurydice was nearing the upper world, "when a sudden frenzy seized Orpheus, unwary in his love, frenzy meet for pardon, did Hell know how to pardon! He stopped, and on the very verge of light, unmindful, alas! and vanquished in purpose, on Eurydice, now his own, looked back! In that moment all his toil was spent, the ruthless tyrant's pact was broken, and thrice a crash was heard amid the pools of Avernus." What means that crash? Surely, that from Nature herself, even in the world below,

"*tears to human suffering are due.*"[107]

That at least is the way a great English poet interprets the line, for Milton doubtless had

[107] Wordsworth, *Laodamia.*

this parallel in view, when, as Eve plucked the fruit,

> "*Earth felt the wound and Nature from her seat*
> *Sighing through all her works gave signs of woe,*
> *That all was lost.*" [108]

At this point, it is worth while to glance afresh at another famous Virgilian scene. It is in the Fourth *Aeneid*.[109] The storm which interrupted the royal hunt has driven Aeneas and Dido to the shelter of the cave. Then, we are told, "primal Earth and nuptial Juno gave the sign; fires flashed in Heaven, the witness to their bridal, and on the mountain-top screamed the Nymphs. That day was the first day of death, that first the cause of woe." Here with poetic art Virgil interprets the phenomena of the storm as if Nature herself were taking part in nuptial ceremonies. Earth and Heaven are active participants; the lightning-fires are marriage-torches; Juno is the *pronuba* or chief attendant on the bride; the cries of mountain-nymphs become the wedding-song. Yet the occasion is far from auspicious, however much Dido may think so. Nature is not in sympathy with her *coniugium*, as she calls it, her *hyme-*

[108] *Paradise Lost*, IX. 780 ff. [109] *Aen.*, IV. 160 ff.

naei, which are merely *incepti.* "That day was the first day of death." This is the scene which would seem to have inspired Milton's second description of Nature's sorrow over the fall of man;

> "*Earth trembled from her entrails, as again*
> *In pangs, and Nature gave a second groan:*
> *Sky lowered, and muttering thunder, some sad drops*
> *Wept at completing of the mortal sin*
> *Original.*" [110]

Sir Archibald Geikie [111] refers to Virgil's silence on mountain-scenery, but I am inclined to think that he has overlooked much of the evidence available. The First *Eclogue* closes with the "longer shadows falling from the mountain-heights," and in the *Georgics,* after the invocation, the first scene is one of "early spring, when icy streams trickle from the snowy mountains." It is an Italian sunrise which the poet describes in the lines, "the morrow's dawn was sprinkling the mountain-tops with light, what time the Sun's steeds first rise from the deep flood, and breathe light from uplifted nostrils," and the brief but beautiful picture of

[110] *Paradise Lost,* IX. 1000 ff.
[111] Geikie, *op. cit.,* pp. 288 ff. and 393.

saxosas inter decurrunt flumina vallis
"streams tumble down amid rocky glens"

is a glimpse into mountain-scenery.[112]

Such scenery includes woods, and glades, and mountain-valleys, and to these there are numerous references. Thus Virgil's happy husbandmen enjoy

latis otia fundis
Speluncae vivique lacus et frigida Tempe
"the ease of broad domains, caverns, and living lakes, and cool vales" [113]

as well as *saltus ac lustra ferarum* ("woodland glades and the haunts of game"), all features such as we are likely to associate in America with Rocky Mountain states like Montana and Colorado, or with the Sierra region of California. It is a mountain stream which Virgil describes, when "rocks delay a rushing river, and there arises a roar from the pent-up flood, and the neighboring banks echo to the plashing waters." [114] Virgil's choice cattle graze in the forests of the high Sila range of Bruttium; the territory which Latinus proposed to give the

[112] *Ecl.*, v. 84. Other citations in the paragraph are from *Ecl.*, I. 83; *Georg.*, I. 43 f. and *Aen.*, XII. 113 ff.
[113] *Georg.*, II. 468 f.
[114] *Aen.*, XI. 297 ff.

Trojans included (perhaps, was to be bounded by) a *celsi plaga pinea montis* ("a pine-clad belt of mountain height"); Camilla, the romantic warrior-maid, worshipped Diana amid the wilds of her Volscian mountains; woods and mountains are the chief features of the young earth, when it first "looks with awe upon the new sun shining above."[115]

Thus Virgil was keenly interested in mountains, though we do not know that he ever actually lived among them. In Italy he knows "Father Apennine himself," who "roaring with quivering oaks, joyously lifts heavenward his snowy head"; he knows Vesuvius and "the heights of Soracte"; he knows Tetrica's rugged crags and Mount Severus; he knows the green ilexes of Mount Alburnus in Lucania; he knows Monte Taburno, which, like "mighty Sila," gives summer grazing to Campanian herds, and Monte Viso, whose "pine-crowned" Ligurian heights shelter wild boars. He knows the Hernican rocks with their dewy streams, and the country of the "cold Anio"; he knows the "groves beneath high Albunea, mightiest of forests, which echoes with hallowed fountain, and breathes forth from her darkness a deadly

[115] *Aen.*, XI. 320; VII. 803 ff., and XI. 843; *Ecl.*, VI. 37 ff.

vapor"; he knows the mysterious Vale of Ampsanctus *Italiae medio sub montibus altis* ("in the heart of Italy, beneath high mountains"); "on either hand a forest's fringe, dark with dense leafage, and in the centre a roaring torrent resounding o'er the rocks in swirling eddies"; he knows, too, "the vast grove, sacred to Silvanus, near Caere's cold stream, widely revered with ancestral awe; on all sides curving hills enclose it, and girdle the woodland with dark fir-trees."[116] Nor should we overlook "the forts on the Noric hills," high up among the "skyey Alps," and the famous hill towns of Italy

Tot congesta manu praeruptis oppida saxis
("*the many towns man's handiwork has piled high on steepy crags*"),

"proud" Tibur, "lofty" Praeneste, "cold" Nursia, "the hills crowned with Collatia's turrets," Agylla, "perched on Etruscan heights," and "mountainous" Nersae, whose Aequian stock "was rugged above all others, and inured to hard hunting in the woods."[117]

[116] *Georg.*, III. 146 f.; *Aen.*, VII. 82 ff., 563 ff., 597 ff., 683 f., 696, 713; X. 708; XII. 701 ff., 715. For the Appennines, cf. Ch. II. above.

[117] *Georg.*, II. 156, 224; III. 474.; *Aen.*, VI. 774; VII. 630, 682, 716, 744 ff.; VIII. 479 f.

In Sicily Virgil knows Mount Eryx, and famous Aetna, whose terrifying eruptions he describes,[118] and as for foreign mountains, though these often involve purely literary associations, they should not be overlooked. They include Athos, known in Italian as Monte Santo; Atlas, which is described in terms of a mountain-god; Cynthos, in Delos, where Apollo himself treads the ridges; Cytorus, towering above the Black Sea and famous for its box-wood; the "lofty" Ceraunia; the "Thunder Peaks" of Epirus; Cithaeron, in Boeotia, which like Spartan Taygetus was the scene of wild Bacchante revels; Gargarus, in the Troad, with rich cornlands on its slopes; Erymanthus, in Arcadia, known for its pines as well as for the boar which Hercules slew; Lycaeus and Maenalus also in Arcadia; Helicon, in Boeotia, and Parnassus, in Phocis, haunts of the Muses; Ida, so familiar from the legends of Troy and Crete; Leucata, with its "storm-capped" Acarnanian peaks; Olympus, Ossa, and Pelion, well-known triumvirate of mountains; the Rhiphaean heights of Scythia; Pindus and Pangaea, Rhodope and the great Balkan (Haemus) range of Thrace.[119]

118 *Aen.*, XII. 701; *Georg.*, I. 472; *Aen.*, III. 570 ff.
119 *Ecl.*, X. 11–15; *Georg.*, I. 16, 103, 281, 332; II. 437,

Mountains are the haunts of Pan, of Nymphs, and of Centaurs, and nowhere is Virgil's feeling for mountain scenery more exquisitely expressed in Greek and Roman terms than in a striking simile in the Seventh *Aeneid,* where he compares the twin brothers from Tibur to "two cloud-born Centaurs, who descend from a mountain's high peak, leaving Homole or snowy Othrys in swift course; the mighty forest yields place as they go, and the thickets give way with a loud crash." [120] "The picture that rises in my mind," writes Warde Fowler,[121] "is that of a mountain range, whose summits are hidden in cloud, below which the snow is visible between the cloud and the pine-forests; below the broad steep slopes of dark pines, the *silva,* are the belts of deciduous trees and underwood (*virgulta*). . . These four stages of the clothing of the mountain seem to me clearly expressed by the poet. First the Centaurs are *nubigenae,* their lair is up there in the clouds; there they were born, and thence they begin their swift descent. . . Secondly, they cross

---

488; III. 11; IV. 462; *Aen.,* III. 274; IV. 147, 246 ff., 303; V. 446.

[120] *Aen.,* VII. 674 ff.; cf. *Georg.,* I. 16 f.; *Aen.,* IV. 168.

[121] *Virgil's "Gathering of the Clans,"* Oxford, 1918, pp. 54 ff.

and leave behind them the stretches of snow below the cloud,

> Homolen Othrymque nivalem
> Linquentes cursu rapido.

Thirdly, they force their way through the pine-woods, the *ingens silva,* but not by tearing up the trees or breaking them down, for the trees give way before them — *dat euntibus ingens silva locum.* Fourthly, once through the broad belts of pine, they come crashing down to the valley through the underwoods, *magno cedunt virgulta fragore,* that is, with noise which those in the valley can now hear plainly." This is indeed a "splendid picture" of mountain scenery which Warde Fowler is perhaps the first of our time to interpret correctly. Virgil and the other great poets of antiquity are not silent about the most imposing aspects of external nature, but modern writers often fail to grasp their meaning, for the ancients did not always pour their thoughts into the same mould as do the nature-poets of our day.

And Virgil's mountains are not without sympathy for man in his joys and sorrows. When Daphnis — representing Julius Caesar in the poet's prophetic fancy — is exalted to the heavens, "the very mountains, with woods unshorn, joyously fling their voices starward; the very rocks, the very groves, ring out the song: 'A god is he, a god, Menalcas!'"[122] Conversely, in the hour when Eurydice died, "her Dryad comrades filled with their cries the mountain-peaks, the towers of Rhodope wept, wept too the Pangaean heights, and the martial land of Rhesus, the Getae and Hebrus and Orithyia, child of Acte."[123] This moving passage, expressive of the grief of Thrace, as voiced by mountains, rivers, nymphs, and people, deserves to be put side by side with those exquisite words, which tell of Nature's lamentation over the death of Umbro, the Marsian snake-charmer and healer:

> Te nemus Angitiae, vitrea te Fucinus unda,
> Te liquidi flevere lacus.

"*Thee Angitia's grove wept, thee Fucinus' glassy wave, thee the limpid lakes!*"[124]

simple words of deepest feeling, in which F. W. Myers found "that accent of brooding sorrow which mourns over the fate of men,

[122] *Ecl.*, v. 62 ff.
[123] *Georg.*, IV. 460 ff.
[124] *Aen.*, VII. 759 f.

and breathes a pathetic murmur into Nature's peace." [125]

Having dealt somewhat fully with Lucretius, whose main theme is Nature herself, and with Virgil, who sings the *divini gloria ruris,* "the glory of the divine country," [126] we do not need for our present purpose to discuss the many other poets of Rome in great detail. Horace, however, the second great poet of the Augustan age, deserves some consideration, partly because of his wide popularity, and partly because his attitude toward nature has occasionally been misinterpreted.

If we may take Horace's own confession, it is the

gelidum nemus
Nympharumque leves cum Satyris chori

"T*he cool of woods, the tripping band*
O*f Nymphs and Satyrs hand in hand*" [127]

that set him apart from the throng for his sacred office. It is the

"*streams that fertile Tibur lave*
A*nd groves that verdant tresses wave*"

that make him the poet he is,

[125] Warde Fowler, *op. cit.*, p. 77.
[126] *Georg.*, I. 168.
[127] *Odes,* I. I. 30 f. (W. S. Morris).

"*The master of th' Aeolian song.*" [128]

He calls himself a *ruris amator*,[129] and in many a poem sets forth the pure and simple joys of the countrymen,

"*Stretched at their ease an hour or so each day*
'Neath arbute green, where quiet fountains play" [130]

and the charm and loveliness of country scenery. In him, says Andrew Lang,[131] "what a sense of all that is fair in the glittering stream, the music of the waterfall, the hum of bees, the silvery grey of the olive woods on the hillside!"

The beauties of Italy are a constant inspiration to the poet. "The sentiment," adds Lang, "is ever in your heart and often on your lips." [132] Tibur, the lovely Tivoli, so familiar to modern tourists, is first in Horace's affection:

"*Others may love Larissa's fertile field,*
Or Lacedaemon with her patient deeds;
To me Albunea's resounding cave,

[128] *Odes,* IV. 3. 10 ff. (John Osborne Sargent and Philip Francis).

[129] *Epistles,* I. 10. 2.

[130] *Odes,* I. I. 30 f. (Translation from *On the Tibur Road* by George Meason Whicher and George Frisbie Whicher, Princeton, 1912.)

[131] Andrew Lang, *Letters to Dead Authors,* p. 228.

[132] *Ibid.,* p. 229.

The groves, the orchards Tibur's rivers lave,
And Anio's falls, a keener pleasure yield." [133]

And next to Tibur come the "happy hills" and the fair streams near Tarentum:

"*No spot so joyous smiles to me*
Of this wide globe's extended shores;
Where nor the labors of the bee
Yield to Hymettus' golden stores,
Nor the green berry of Venafran soil
Swells with a riper flood of fragrant oil.

There Jove his kindest gifts bestows,
There joys to crown the fertile plains,
With genial warmth the winter glows
And spring with lengthen'd honors reigns,
Nor Aulon, friendly to the clustering vine,
Envies the vintage of Falernian wine.

That happy place, that sweet retreat,
The charming hills, that round it rise,
Your latest hours and mine await,
And when at length your Horace dies,
There the deep sigh thy poet-friend shall mourn,
And pious tears bedew his glowing urn." [134]

It is Horace who gives us this picture of Apollo:

[133] *Odes,* I. 7. 11 ff. ("Horatian Echoes" by John Osborne Sargent).
[134] *Odes,* II. 6. 13 ff. (Philip Francis).

"*Whose bow is on his shoulders ever laid,*
Who bathes his flowing locks in crystal dew
Of Castaly, who Lycia's thickets haunts,—
and who
Finds home and altar in his native glade,"[135]

He sings too of Diana, "queen of the woods," as *laetam fluviis et nemorum coma,* "delighting in streams and leafage of groves," and to her dedicates the pine that overlooks his country house.[136]

Pan, known to Italians as Faunus, haunts Horace's "lovely" Lucretilis, and inspires a hymn, which reveals the poet's delightful sympathy with his neighbors' rustic faith, for on the December day hallowed to Faunus the powers of evil are at rest — wild beasts will do no harm — and the woods pay homage to their god:

"*Sportive the herd through grassy meadow flees,*
The ox is pastured, and the folk at ease
Maintain thy winter-festival; grown bold,
The sheep fear not the wolf within the fold;
Woods yield their boughs to grace thy holiday;
And delvers gaily stamp the hated clay."[137]

[135] *Odes,* III. 4. 60 ff.
[136] *Odes,* I. 21. 5, *Carmen Saeculare,* I, and *Odes,* III. 22.
[137] *Odes,* III. 18 (*On the Tibur Road* by G. M. and G. F. Whicher, p. 31).

It is Horace who loves

" *My little copse, my brook so fair to see,*
My faithful harvest — no such happy lot
Is his who holds rich Africa in fee,
Although he knows it not," [138]

and who asks why man should not enjoy the charms of nature:

" *Else wherefore do the pine-trees slim*
And poplar white enlace their sprays
In kindly shade? Why frets the stream
To wimple down its winding ways? " [139]

It is Horace too who by the magic of his verse has made an Italian fountain as well known in literature as any of the famous springs of Greece,

O fons Bandusiae, splendidior vitro

where

" *The Dog-star with his fiercest beam*
Can never touch thy shaded stream,
Cool refuge for the weary ox
With ploughing spent, and roaming flocks.

'Mid founts of fame thou too shalt be,
What time I sing the ilex tree

[138] *Odes,* III. 16. 29 ff. (W. S. Marris, Oxford, 1912).
[139] *Odes,* II. 3. 9 ff. (W. S. Marris).

That overhangs the grotto deep
From which thy babbling waters leap." [140]

And yet, in spite of the ample evidence to the contrary, we find Professor Postgate asserting that Horace was essentially a townsman who derived no inspiration from the country.[141] We must be content to let the poet speak for himself. We have already cited his rhapsody upon Tarentum,[142] and we later find him likening his beloved country-seat to the same beautiful region and speaking of it in such terms as these:

Hae latebrae dulces, etiam, si credis, amoenae
" *This retreat, so charming, yes, believe me, so bewitching* " [143]

Here the stronger epithet *amoenae*, implying personal enthusiasm, and strikingly contrasted with the milder epithet *dulces*, which implies mere charm, is the same that Horace uses elsewhere of the country scenes which to his bailiff were merely *deserta et inhospita tesqua*, " desert and inhospitable wilds." [144] It

140 *Odes*, III. 13 (W. S. Marris).
141 See Duff's *A Literary History of Rome*, p. 539.
142 See p. 228 above.
143 *Epist.*, I. 16. 11 and 15.
144 *Epist.*, I. 14. 19 f. Cf. vs. 10, 16 f. and *Odes*, I. 17. 1 f.

is the same epithet which is applied to the beloved Monte Gennaro, *amoenum Lucretilem*, one of Pan's favorite haunts. "I call him happy," adds Horace, "who lives in the country and I depart in gloom, whenever hateful business drags me off to Rome." He is *solibus aptus*,[145] a lover of the sun, and is always glad to get away from

"T*he dust and din and steam of town*,"

a familiar line of Tennyson's which echoes Horace's famous

Fumum et opes strepitumque Romae.[146]

But even a stranger departure from rational criticism is that indulged in by Professor Tyrrell, who finds in the pleasing picture of rural contentment in the Second *Epode* "a clear proof of the poet's insensibility to these pleasures" of country life.[147] In this interesting piece of satire we have a rich usurer's dream of rural bliss, which can not be realized because his money-grubbing instincts are too strong. Tyr-

[145] *Epist.*, I. 20. 24.

[146] *Odes*, III. 29. 12. Cf. Tennyson, *In Memoriam*, 89.

[147] *Latin Poetry*, by Robert Yelverton Tyrrell, Boston, 1895. Tyrrell's criticisms of Horace are answered in detail by the present writer in "A Defense of Horace" in *The Classical Journal*, XI. 454 ff. (1915-16).

rell cites as a parallel Calverley's amusing skit about "the city clerk who left the heat and noise and brass bands of Camden Hill to enjoy his well-earned holiday. We read how he laughed when he felt the cool breeze fanning his cheek and the soft spray on his lip, and when all the sights and sounds and fragrances of the country were wafted to him; then how, when he remembered the dusty streets he had left,

> "*at the thought*
> H*e laughed again, and softly drew*
> T*hat 'Morning Herald,' that he'd brought,*
> F*orth from his breast, and read it through!*"

Is it a fair inference that Calverley (or for that matter even the city clerk) was indifferent to the delights of the country and seashore? Yet that is precisely how Tyrrell draws his preposterous conclusion about Horace, to whose youthful imagination we owe the cheerful portrait of the happy husbandman (*beatus ille*), from which we may quote some portions: [148]

> "L*ike the first mortals bless'd is he,*
> F*rom debts, and usury, and business free*
> W*ith his own team who ploughs the soil,*
> W*hich grateful once confess'd his father's toil.*

[148] *Epodes*, ii.

Sometimes his marriageable vines
Around the lofty bridgegroom elm he twines;
Or lops the vagrant boughs away,
Ingrafting better as the old decay;
Or in the vale with joys surveys
His lowing herd safe-wandering as they graze;
Or careful stores the flowing gold
Press'd from the hive, or shears his tender fold;
Or when with various fruits o'erspread,
The mellow Autumn lifts his beauteous head,
His grafted pears or grapes, that vie
With the rich purple of the Tyrian dye,
Grateful he gathers, and repays
His guardian gods upon their festal days:
Sometimes beneath an ancient shade,
Or on the matted grass supinely laid,
Where pours the mountain stream along,
And feather'd warblers chant the soothing song;
Or where the lucid fountain flows,
And with its murmurs courts him to repose." [149]

In this Second *Epode*, therefore, we have no reason to think that Horace is ridiculing the nature-poetry of his day. In the *Ars Poetica*, however, he has a fling at "purple patches," and these he illustrates by reference to descriptions — doubtless from contemporary verse — such as portray Diana's grove and altar,

[149] Translation by Philip Francis.

"*The winding stream a-speeding 'mid fair fields,*"

the river Rhine, and a rainbow.[150]

But perhaps the most distinctive evidence of Horace's love of nature, and of his longing for detachment from the life of crowds and cities is to be found in a passage which is too commonly misinterpreted. In his early manhood, when in the train of Brutus, Horace had visited famous cities of Asia, and at a much later date he writes to Bullatius, a friend who is making the same *grand tour:* [151] "What did you think of Chios, my Bullatius, and of famous Lesbos? What of charming Samos? What of Sardis, royal home of Croesus? What of Smyrna and Colophon? Whether above or below their fame, do they all seem poor beside the Campus and Tiber's stream? Or is your heart set upon one of the cities of Attalus? Or do you extol Lebedus, because sick of sea and road? You know what Lebedus is — a town more desolate than Gabii or Fidenae: yet there would I love to live, and, forgetting my friends and by them forgotten, gaze from the land on Neptune's distant rage." Some editors suppose that the last lines of this passage, instead of expressing

150 *Ars Poetica,* 14 ff.
151 *Epist.,* I. 11.

Horace's own sentiments, are cited from a letter of Bullatius, written to the poet. But there is absolutely nothing to indicate that the words are a quotation. Rather have we here a record of Horace's own experience. The angry sea, beating upon the shore at lonely Lebedus, had fascinated him years before, and he would be glad to live in such a picturesque spot,

"*The world forgetting, by the world forgot,*"

for to Horace, as to Lucretius, it was

> Suave, mari magno turbantibus aequora ventis,
> E terra . . . spectare.

Thus "old popular Horace" can here across the centuries clasp hands with Byron, for to both

> "*There is a rapture in the lonely shore,*
> *There is society, where none intrudes,*
> *By the deep Sea, and music in its roar.*" [152]

The Roman elegiac poets must be disposed of more summarily than they deserve. Among the friends of Horace was Albius Tibullus, who, while still very young, died in the same year as Virgil. "What are you doing," writes Horace to him,[153] "in your country at Pedum?

[152] *Childe Harold,* IV. 178.

[153] *Epist.,* I. 4. I accept the view that the Albius of

Writing? Or strolling peacefully amid the healthful woods, musing on all that is worthy of one wise and good?" This kindly letter of the older poet very appropriately suggests to us the gentle, meditative character of one who has left us some charming idyllic pictures of country life which are not unworthy to be placed side by side with scenes that we have studied in the older literature. "The sight of corn-fields and vineyards, of hills and plains, with the added charm of animal life, gives him the pleasure which it gives to Virgil and Lucretius, and to Horace in his more idyllic moods; and the elegies abound with evidence that those were the sights most constantly before him, and those which sank into his heart.[154]

As to Propertius, he describes the country of his birth with careful detail. "Ancient Umbria bore thee in a home of high renown . . . where misty Mevania sheds its dews on the hollow plain and the waters of Umbria's lake send

---

this Epistle is the poet Tibullus. Literature on this disputed point is cited on p. 275 of my *Horace: Satires, Epistles, and Ars Poetica,* in *The Loeb Classical Library,* 1926.

154 "Horace and the Elegiac Poets" in Sellar's *The Roman Poets of the Augustan Age,* p. 247.

forth their summer steam, and the wall rises from the peak of climbing Asis."[155] He can sing the glories of nature unadorned: "See what hues lovely earth sends forth; 'tis the wild ivy springs fairest ever; loveliest the arbutus that grows in the caverns of the wilderness, and all untaught are the channels where the waters run. Begemmed with native pebbles the shores beguile our eyes, and birds sing sweetlier from their lack of art."[156] He is glad to have his beloved Cynthia alone in the country, and gaze on lonely mountains, on flocks and a poor farmer's lands,

> Sola eris et solos spectabis, Cynthia, montes
> Et pecus et fines pauperis agricolae,[157]

not, however, that she may commune with nature, but that she may be removed from the temptations and luxury of the town. Thus mountains have no attraction for him, and the *vesani murmura ponti*, "the murmurs of the raging sea,"[158] suggest only peril for sea-faring people.

In Ovid we have the greatest *raconteur* in

[155] *Propertius,* IV. I. 121 ff. The translation used is by H. E. Butler, in *The Loeb Classical Library,* 1916.
[156] *Propertius,* I. 2. 9 ff. (Butler).
[157] *Propertius,* II. 19. 7 f.
[158] *Propertius,* I. 8. 5.

Latin literature, who would seem likely to yield us ample material to illustrate our theme. He was born high up in the Paelignian country at Sulmo, through which wander streams of water, while green plants thrive in the tender soil. " 'Tis a land rich in corn and richer still in the grape; here and there its fields bring forth, too, the berry-bearing tree of Pallas; and over the mead whose herbage ever springs again along the gliding streams, the grassy turf hides thickly the moistened ground." [159]

In Ovid's voluminous verse we have many vivid descriptions of scenery, more or less fanciful, which would please us more if we did not suspect that they are ornamental pictures and nothing more. Ovid, in fact, is the best representative of purely descriptive poetry in all antiquity. Take as an illustration his account of the sacred spring near Hymettus, as translated by Sir Archibald Geikie:[160]

" *Near to Hymettus with its flowery slopes*
A sacred spring lies, borded with soft turf,
In the low copsewood of a shady grove.
The arbute overspreads the verdant sward;

[159] Ovid, *Amores,* II. 16. 5 ff. (Translation by Grant Showerman, in *The Loeb Classical Library,* 1914.)

[160] Ovid, *Ars Amat.,* III. 687 ff. (Geikie's *Love of Nature Among the Romans,* p. 103.)

The air around is fragrant with the scents
Of laurels, rosemary, and myrtles dark;
Nor is the box-tree absent, with its leafage dense,
Nor fragile tamarisk, nor cytisus,
Beneath the shadow of the garden pine.
Stirred by the zephyrs with their balmy breath,
The boughs above wave gently to and fro,
The taller grasses quiver underneath."

Such descriptions are numerous and illustrate Ovid's romantic vein, but we fail to find in him the sincerity of feeling and the real sympathy with nature which we instinctively associate with Virgil and less so with Horace. And yet Ovid's influence on later literature is immense, and no little of the interest in nature found in mediaeval romance is traceable directly to him. We should note too that, while Ovid often brings before us Nymphs and Fauns and other woodland deities, yet he does not really feel their presence, for they have become to him as purely traditional and conventional as they are to the average poet of to-day.

Among the poets of Rome's Silver Age we may glance at only a few. Thus Statius in his *Silvae* gives us some interesting sketches of country-houses at such lovely spots as Tivoli and Sorrento.[161] Of the villa of Vopiscus at Tibur he writes: "How beautiful beyond human art the enchanted scene! Nowhere has Nature more lavishly spent her skill. Lofty woods lean over rushing waters; a false image counterfeits the foliage, and the reflection dances unbroken over the long waves. Anio himself — marvellous to believe — though full of boulders below and above, here silences his swollen rage and foamy din, as if afraid to disturb the Pierian days and music-haunted slumbers of tranquil Vopiscus."[162] And yet, as Duff puts it, "To come from a simple and direct kind of poetry to Statius is like passing out of the open breeze into a conservatory of flowers, where many are beautiful but many raise the conviction that they are forced."[163] Statius has developed the Alexandrian taste for pictures, and his love of painting and other forms of art has led him into over-refinement, and an excessive use of ornamentation. His scenery, adds Duff, is not unlike that of Watteau's *Fêtes Champêtres*.

[161] Statius, *Silvae*, II. 2.

[162] *Silvae*, I. 3. 15 ff. (Translation by J. H. Mozley, in *The Loeb Classical Library*, 1928.)

[163] J. Wight Duff: *A Literary History of Rome in the Silver Age*, London, 1927, p. 493.

Martial, a close contemporary of Statius, but born in Spain, has won fame with his great collection of witty and polished epigrams. In these he often shows a deep appreciation of rural aspects and a poet's eye for landscape beauties. He is fond of flowers and garlands, and names [164] the chief places in Italy where roses flourished best — Paestum and Tibur, Tusculum and Praeneste, Campania and his own Nomentum, but it is Virgil's *biferi rosaria Paesti* [165] that win his special praise, for with the roses of Paestum Egypt can not compete:

"*Let not thy winters, Nile, then vie with ours,*
Go plough, and send us corn; we'll send thee flow'rs." [166]

He describes with pride a great plane-tree at Cordova, planted by Julius Caesar:

"*Under that shade the rusticke Dryades*
And wanton Fauns themselves with sporting please;
And oft, as she by night from Pan doth fly,
This silent house doth Syrinx terrifie.
There oft hath Bacchus kept his revelling
When wine has made the tree more richly spring.

164 *Martial,* IX. 60.
165 *Virgil, Georgics,* IV. 119.
166 *Martial,* VI. 80 (Anonymous, 1695).

There roses grow t' adorne the drinking
crowne;
And none can say those roses are his owne." [167]

Here his romantic fancy peoples the shadows with Fauns and Dryads, just as in a poem [168] written after the great eruption of Vesuvius in 79 A.D., he pictures the mountain-slopes, now utterly desolate, as lately the home of Bacchus, the Satyrs, Venus and Hercules.[169]

"*Vesuvius, cover'd with the fruitful vine,*
Here flourish'd once, and ran with floods of wine:
Here Bacchus oft to the cool shades retired,
And his own native Nysa less admired:
Oft to the mountain's airy tops advanced,
The frisking Satyrs on the summits danced:
Alcides here, here Venus, graced the shore,
Nor loved her favorite Lacedaemon more.
Now piles of ashes, spreading all around
In undistinguish'd heaps, deform the ground.
The gods themselves the ruin'd seats bemoan,
And blame the mischiefs that themselves have
done." [170]

Martial's friend Juvenal was too intent on writing satires upon the foibles of mankind to

[167] *Martial,* IX. 61 (May).
[168] *Martial,* IV. 44.
[169] Venus and Hercules were the deities of Pompeii and Herculaneum respectively.
[170] The translation is by Addison.

give much attention to external nature. He does, however, pause once to observe how superior nature is to art. At the spring of Egeria, banked up with slabs of precious marble, he exclaims,

> "*How much more near*
> W*ould be the fountain nymph, if simple grass*
> E*nclosed the waters with its margent green,*
> N*or marble kerb profaned the native stone;*"[171]

and in another unexpected verse he prays that the last resting place of those who in better days reverenced their teachers may rejoice in the "breath of the crocus and in an endless spring."[172]

The *perpetuum ver* of Juvenal serves as a stepping-stone as we pass to one of the loveliest poems in the Latin language, which may well be called a Hymn of Spring.

> Cras amet qui numquam amavit quique amavit cras amet;
> Ver novum, ver iam canorum, ver renatus orbis est;
> Vere concordant amores, vere nubunt alites,
> Et nemus comam resolvit de maritis imbribus.

[171] *Juvenal,* III. 18 ff. (Translation by J. D. Duff, Cambridge, 1925.)
[172] *Juvenal,* VI. 208.

Cras amet qui numquam amavit quique amavit
cras amet.

. . .

"*Tomorn who ne'er hath loved shall love, and who hath loved shall love tomorn.*
Spring is young, spring now is chanting, spring is all the world reborn.
Love in spring is knit to love, bird weds with bird in springtide hours,
And the wood unbinds her rippling tresses under nuptial showers.
Tomorn who ne'er hath loved shall love, and who hath loved shall love tomorn." [173]

This *Pervigilium Veneris* is anonymous and can not be dated with certainty, but is commonly associated with the revival, under Hadrian, of the worship of Venus Genetrix. Its tone, however, is indicative of a much later date. Written in trochaic septenarii, the poem approximates to accentual rhythm, and is characterized by the free use of assonance, and even of occasional rhyme. As to substance, it is a wonderful outburst of exalted joy at the coming of that season of spring which was linked with the Queen of Love and

[173] From *Sappho and the Vigil of Venus,* translated by A. S. Way, London, 1920.

Beauty.[174] It is the spirit of Horace's

Iam Cytherea choros ducit Venus,[175]

combined with that of Botticelli's "*Spring*," only the feeling is no longer held in classic restraint, but is poured forth in the full stream of romantic fervor.

"Lo, *the crimson-flushing petals have unveiled the blush of shame,*
And from glowing clusters now is flashing forth the roses' flame."

"The Eve of St. Venus," as Professor Mackail translates the title, is an early herald of a new age of life and thought, yet unborn.[176]

Another poem which stands on the borderland between classicism and romance is the interesting *Mosella* of Ausonius, written about 370 A.D. The writer, born at Bordeaux, and of professorial standing at its University, opens with a brief sketch of a journey he had made from Bingen to Neumagen. Here "the whole

[174] Compare the famous invocation of Venus in Lucretius. See pp. 17 and 189 above.

[175] *Odes*, I. 4. 5, and see p. 28 above.

[176] J. W. Mackail's prose translation is given in the same volume with Catullus and Tibullus in *The Loeb Classical Library*, 1912. Probably the best verse translation in English is by Fort, in quatrains, Oxford, 1922, but at the time of writing I am not able to consult a copy.

gracious prospect made me behold a picture of my own native land, the smiling and well-tended country of Bordeaux — the roofs of country-houses, perched high upon the over-hanging river-banks, the hill-sides green with vines, and the pleasant stream of Moselle gliding below with subdued murmuring."[177]

Here follows an address to the Moselle,

> Salve, amnis laudate agris, laudate colonis

> "*Hail, O river, renowned for thy fields, renowned for thy husbandmen*"

> "River, whose hills are o'ergrown with Bacchus' fragrant vines, o'ergrown, river most verdant, thy banks with turf: ship-bearing as the sea, with sloping waters gliding as a river, and with thy crystal depths the peer of lakes, brooks thou canst match for hurrying flow, cool springs surpass for limpid draughts; one, thou hast all that belongs to springs, brooks, rivers, lakes, and tidal Ocean with his ebb and flow."[178]

Then comes an Homeric catalogue, not of men, but of fish, in their many kinds and names, and since "it is not lawful for the poet to declare" them, he prevails upon the Nymph, "who

[177] Ausonius, *Mosella,* 18 ff. (Translation by Hugh G. Evelyn-White, in *The Loeb Classical Library,* 1919).

[178] *Mosella,* 23 ff. (Evelyn-White).

dwells in the river's realm" to discourse upon so learned a theme. After fish come the vine-clad hills round about and the busy husbandmen upon the slopes, and the divine beings that throng river and hills alike — Satyrs and Nymphs, Pans and Fauns and Oreads, all engaged in merry frolic. Aquatic sports and the fishing-throngs are the next topic, to be followed by a description of the noble mansions lining the banks, and of the river's tributary streams. The poem — 483 verses — concludes with an apostrophe of the Moselle, which henceforth "shall pass upon the lips of men and be cherished with joyful song."

The *Mosella,* an attractive, if somewhat overrated poem, is exceptional as an epic of description and personal experience, yet in its details it is so obviously imitative, that it gives one the impression, not of an original poem, but of a cento of poems. One of its most striking passages deals with the reflections of the hills in the clear water: "Yon is a sight that may be freely enjoyed: when the azure river mirrors the shady hill, the waters of the stream seem to bear leaves and the flood to be all o'ergrown with shoots of vines. What a hue is on the waters when Hesperus has driven forward the lagging shadows and o'erspread Moselle with the green of the reflected height! Whole hills float on the shivering ripples: here quivers the far-off tendril of the vine, here in the glassy flood swells the full cluster. The deluded boatman tells o'er the green vines — the boatman whose skiff of bark floats on the watery floor out in mid-stream, where the pictured hill blends with the river and where the river joins with the edges of the shadows." [179] This passage, as Mr. Evelyn-White reminds us, is imitated by Pope in his description of the Loddon:

> "*Oft in her glass the musing shepherd spies*
> *The headlong mountains and the downward skies,*
> *The wat'ry landscape of the pendent woods,*
> *And absent trees that tremble in the floods;*
> *In the clear azure gleam the flocks are seen,*
> *And floating forests paint the waves with green.*" [180]

The Ausonius passage is developed from the ideas in Virgil's lines describing the voyage of Aeneas up the tranquil Tiber: "over the waters glides the well-pitched pine; in wonder the waves, in wonder unwonted woods view the far

[179] *Mosella,* 189 ff. (Evelyn-White).
[180] Pope, *Windsor Forest,* 211 ff.

gleaming shields of warriors and the painted hulls floating on the stream. They with their rowing give night and day no rest, pass the long bends, are shaded with diverse trees, and cleave the green woods in the peaceful water." [181]

Undoubtedly, Ausonius does possess a "romantic sense of the beauties of nature," and, in view of the love he shows for the northland of his birth, Mackail does well to rank him "not merely as the last, or all but the last, of Latin, but as the first of French poets." [182] Claudian and Rutilius Namatianus continue for a few years longer the imperial tradition,[183] but with them purely Roman poetry comes to an end. It is an absolutely new note that is now first heard in Christian hymns, which take little account of merely terrestrial glories, but transfer us to that other world foreshadowed by Virgil, where "an ampler ether clothes the meads with roseate light, and they know their own sun, and stars of their own." [184]

[181] Virgil, *Aeneid,* VIII. 91 ff.

[182] Mackail, *Latin Literature,* p. 266.

[183] Claudian, author of *The Rape of Proserpina,* died about 404 A.D.; Rutilius Claudius Namatianus wrote his *De Reditu Suo* in 416 A.D.

[184] *Aeneid,* VI. 640 f.

X. EPILOGUE

THE abundant evidence which can thus be drawn from various sources — mythology, religion, philosophy, art, and literature — proves conclusively that the ancient Greeks and Romans did not differ essentially from modern people in their appreciation of the world of nature. We may indeed distinguish different tones at different times, such as the naïve feeling for nature in Homer, a sympathetic feeling, which is more conspicuous in lyric poetry and in drama, and the romantic feeling, which, first developed in a pronounced way by Euripides, is especially prominent in Alexandrian and Roman imperial times, but all the varied tones that are heard in English literature, whether in Chaucer and Shakespeare, in the eighteenth century, in Wordsworth and the Victorians, or in our most recent poetry, can all be detected in the various phases of Greek and Roman thought.

Remembering that the ancients did not always express themselves in terms similar to ours, we must learn to interpret them, and we shall find that often in mythological allusions and artistic symbolism they are expressing a sincere appreciation of nature's beauties and marvels. Their literature alone, howevei, furnishes an immense amount of positive testimony as to their attitude toward nature, and this testimony is naturally best understood by the scientific age in which we live.

But it is sometimes asserted that a lack of interest in nature is admitted by the ancients themselves. Thus Plato's *Critias* has been cited to show that in the fourth century B.C. people were quick to discern defects in an artist's portrayal of the human form, but were quite satisfied with "a sort of indistinct and deceptive mode of shadowing forth" landscape features.[1] But all that this passage proves is that in Plato's day the art of sculpture was more advanced than the art of landscape-painting, which did not mature until the late Hellenistic period.

So, too, in the *Phaedrus*,[2] Socrates, it is said,

[1] Plato, *Critias*, 107B (Jowett). Cited by Butcher, *Some Aspects of the Greek Genius*, p. 253 (3d ed.), and by W. R. Hardie, *Lectures on Classical Subjects*, London, 1903, p. 9.
[2] Plato, *Phaedrus*, 227–230. (Jowett).

disclaims any interest in the beauty of the place to which his friend has led him. Unlike the Duke in the forest of Arden, for whom

> "*this our life, exempt from public haunt,*
> *Finds tongues in trees, books in the running brooks,*
> *Sermons in stones, and good in everything,*"[3]

Socrates makes the announcement: "I am a lover of knowledge, and the men who dwell in the city are my teachers, and not the trees, or the country." But this is largely dramatic, for a perusal of the passage as a whole shows first, that Phaedrus at least takes a peculiar interest in the natural beauties of the place, and secondly, that Socrates himself is far from indifferent to them.

When first encountered by Socrates, Phaedrus was about to take a walk outside the city-walls, for their friend Acumenus had assured him that it would be "far more refreshing than walking in the courts." Upon this Socrates suggests that they go to the Ilissus and there sit down at some quiet spot. Phaedrus leads the way along the brook, for it is cooling to their feet, and "at mid-day and in the summer is far from unpleasant." They then make for

[3] *As You Like It*, II. I. 15 ff.

the tallest plane-tree, where they find " shade and gentle breezes and grass." Hereupon Phaedrus, inspired by a beautiful old myth, asks Socrates if that is not the very spot where Boreas is said to have carried off Orithyia from the banks of the Ilissus. " The little stream is delightfully clear and bright; I can fancy that there might be maidens playing near " (each " full beautiful, a faery's child? "). Thus Phaedrus is in a highly romantic mood, from which the cold philosopher must call him back to reality, for he hasn't time to discuss incredible myths, but must go about the business laid upon him by the Delphian oracle, when it said, " Know thyself." And yet it is Socrates himself who shows great delight in the beautiful scene to which he has been led, and who thus describes its charms: " Yes, indeed, and a fair and shady resting-place, full of summer sounds and scents. There is the lofty and spreading plane-tree, and the agnus castus high and clustering, in the fullest blossom and the greatest fragrance; and the stream which flows beneath the plane-tree is deliciously cold to the feet. Judging from the ornaments and images, this must be a spot sacred to Achelous and the Nymphs; moreover, there is a sweet breeze, and the grasshoppers chirrup; and the greatest charm of all is the grass like a pillow gently sloping to the head. My dear Phaedrus, you have been an admirable guide." The passage as a whole, with its allusion to Achelous and the Nymphs, strikingly illustrates the popular attitude toward the beauties of water and woods, and assures us not only that Phaedrus is inspired by these charms, but also that even Socrates can not utterly suppress their emotional appeal.

Turning from Plato to Cicero, we might cite numerous passages where the Roman philosopher-statesman indulges in rhapsodies upon the marvels of the physical universe. One of the most impressive of these is in the first book of the *Tusculan Disputations*,[4] where the writer, claiming that the soul of man is akin to God himself, plunges into this eloquent outburst: "When we see first the beauty and the brightness of the sky, then the amazing speed, which our thought can not grasp, of its revolution, next the succession of day and night and the changes of the seasons divided into four to suit the ripening of the fruits of the earth and the con-

[4] Cicero, *Tusculan Disputations*, I. 28. 68–70. Translation by J. E. King, in *The Loeb Classical Library*, 1927.

stitution of living bodies, and the sun their ruler and guide, and the moon marking as it were and indicating the days in the calendar by the waxing and waning of her light, . . and the aspect of the heavens at night decked everywhere with stars, . . and here, where we live, there cease not in due season

> *Skies to be shining and trees in leaf blossoming,*
> *Tendrils of joy-giving vines to be burgeoning,*
> *Foison of berries the boughs to be burdening,*
> *Fields to be rich with crops, flowers out everywhere,*
> *Fountains to bubble and grasses the meads cover,*

when then we behold all these things and countless others, can we doubt that some being is over them?" In other words, says Cicero, both the stars above and the trees and flowers below declare,

> "*The Hand that made us is divine.*"

In such a passage Cicero is not unworthy to be compared with the speaker in Ecclesiasticus:

> "*I will make mention now of the works of the Lord,*
> *And will declare the things that I have seen:*
> *In the words of the Lord are his works.*
> *The sun that giveth light looketh upon all things;*
> *And the work of the Lord is full of his glory.*"

Pliny the Younger lives on a more mundane plane than Cicero in the above passage, but his love of nature is outspoken. In the peaceful retreat of his Laurentine villa, he finds what he longs for, the *recta sinceraque vita;* and so, in his ardent enthusiasm, he exclaims:[5] *O mare, O litus, verum secretumque quam multa invenitis, quam multa dictatis!* ("O sea, O shore, true haunt of the Muses, withdrawn from the world, how much you inspire, how much you prompt me to write!") This power of nature to inspire thought and utterance — so familiar to all writers — is implied in these well-known lines of Wordsworth:

"I *heard a thousand blended notes,*
W*hile in a grove I sate reclined,*
I*n that sweet mood when pleasant thoughts*
B*ring sad thoughts to the mind.*"

The pleasure which Pliny found in nature he claims unreservedly as he sends a friend an account of some floating islands: "there is nothing that gives either you or me as much pleasure as the works of nature."[6]

As to the comparative absence of descriptive matter which a reader of the Classics must often observe in the writings before him, it is to

[5] Pliny, *Epistles,* I. 9. 6. [6] *Ibid.* VIII. 20. 10.

be remembered that great authors, whether ancient or modern, often show marked restraint in speaking of subjects that must lie close to their hearts. Let us recall what Coleridge once said about Shakespeare: "Shakespeare never gives a description of rustic scenery merely for its own sake, or to show how well he can paint natural objects: he is never tedious or elaborate; but while he now and then displays marvellous accuracy and minuteness of knowledge, he usually only touches upon the larger features and broader characteristics, leaving the fillings up to the imagination. Thus, in *As You Like It,* he describes an oak of many centuries' growth in a single line —

"*Under an oak, whose antique root peeps out.*"

Other and inferior writers would have dwelt on this description, and worked it out with all the pettiness and impertinence of detail. In Shakespeare, the 'antique' root furnishes the whole picture." [7]

This principle should not be overlooked when we consider the attitude of the ancients toward mountain scenery, for it is worth while

[7] Quoted by William J. Rolfe, in his edition of *As You Like It.*

observing that however seldom we find mountains described in their literature, both Greeks and Romans lived among them or at least in sight of them. The natural glory of Greece is its diversified scenery; "mountains with their bases plunged into the sea, valleys intersected by great rivers, rich plains and meadows inlaid between the hill-ranges, deeply indented shores, promontories, wood-clad or temple-crowned looking out over the many-islanded Aegean;"[8] and as for Italy, the Alps, or the Apennines, or lesser ranges, always dominate the landscape, and a visitor going to Italy from a country where mountains are seldom seen is never unconscious of their presence. Yet both Greeks and Romans often seem indifferent to this, the grandest feature of their countries.

Notwithstanding this reticence in their literature, we nevertheless possess some positive and convincing evidence of a deep appreciation of mountain scenery among the ancients. If, says Gildersleeve,[9] one is disposed to think that "the Greeks did not have the same appreciation of scenery that moderns have, . . a visit

[8] J. C. Shairp, *On Poetic Interpretation of Nature,* Boston, 1896, p. 142.

[9] *The American Journal of Philology,* XXXIV. 492 (1913).

to the sites of Greek temples would forever dispel such nonsense," and Gilbert Murray writes:[10] "They did not describe forests and mountains; they worshipped them and built temples in them. Their love of nature was that of the mountaineer and seaman, who does not talk much about sea or mountain, but sickens and pines if he is taken away from them."

In an article on "The Mountains of Greece"[11] Professor Hyde has brought together a great deal of scientific and aesthetic information upon this interesting subject, and in another article, published in the same year, on "The Ancient Appreciation of Mountain Scenery,"[12] he repeats his assurance that "the intimate sympathy and love for their varied natural surroundings," which the Greeks possessed, "is actually shown by the wealth of legend which haunted every part of their land; and the picturesque location of many a temple on sea cliff, mountain side and in romantic woodland makes it impossible not to believe that they

[10] "Greek and English Tragedy" (Introduction), in *English Literature and the Classics* (Ed., G. S. Gordon), 1912.

[11] *Bulletin of the Geographical Society of Philadelphia,* XIII. (1915).

[12] In *The Classical Journal,* XI. 70–84 (1915–16).

were possessed of a developed sense of natural beauty." This observation about the picturesque sites of temples is happily supplemented by Dr. Robert C. Horn,[13] who remarks that the theatres also "for the most part are in the most striking positions, so that the spectators enjoyed a view of surpassing loveliness or grandeur." He instances the theatre of Dionysus at Athens and the theatres of Epidaurus and Syracuse. "But the two most charming and inspiring sites for theatres are those at Taormina, the ancient Tauromenium, and Delphi. The former, with its view of changing sea, the low, green plains, and Aetna in the background, its head crowned with snow, affords a riot of natural color and form. . . At Delphi, one is struck by the grandeur of the view. . . For my part, I think it impossible for men to have chosen just that place for a theatre and to have constructed it just as it is, without having been influenced in their choice by the appeal of natural beauty and grandeur."

Finally, as regards the ancient attitude toward such aspects of nature as the sea and mountains, let us not over-emphasize the frequent references in Greek and Roman writers

[13] *Ibid.*, p. 302.

to the cold, or hardships, or dangers of seafaring and mountain-travel. It is not reasonable, for instance, to take Livy's famous account of Hannibal's daring passage of the Alps, or the poetic description of the same episode in Silius, as proof that the Romans could see nothing but horrors in the mountains. If Caesar, while crossing the same mountains, could calmly compose a work on language, he may have been indifferent to mountain scenery, but he was certainly not frightened by it, and the remark of Cicero[14] that "if we have dwelt some time amid mountains and forests we take delight in them" expresses a general truth that is just as applicable in our day as it was in his. *Omne ignotum pro magnifico,* "the unknown is ever magnified."[15]

The conditions of travel in modern times, made wonderfully comfortable and easy, are essentially different from those of antiquity, when men had to face perils from wild beasts, "perils of waters, perils of robbers, perils in the wilderness,"[16] and it is not surprising if Greek and Roman travellers, however much they may

[14] *De Amicitia,* XIX. 68.

[15] Tacitus, *Agricola,* ch. XXX. Translation by Maurice Hutton, in *The Loeb Classical Library,* 1914.

[16] St. Paul, 2 *Corin.* XI. 26.

have appreciated beauty and grandeur of scenery, were inclined to dwell more upon *modo silvarum ac montium profunda, modo tempestatum ac fluctuum adversa,* "forest-depths and mountain-heights on the one side, the trials of tempests and of seas on the other." [17] In the sixteenth century, the sea at Dover was to Edmund Spenser "Horrible, hideous, roaring with hoarse crie." Modern writers still give us vivid pictures of the dangers and difficulties of travel. The sea can still sound "the eternal note of sadness," can still inspire horror:

> "*Find me one grave of thy thousand graves,*
> *Those pure cold populous graves of thine,*" [18]

and as for the mountains, do we not all know people for whom those wondrous heights are "a chaos dread," [19] spelling depression of spirits and a melancholy mood? "Very beautiful, but rather terrifying," is Madam Waddington's remark about crossing Mont Cenis, and "sinistres" is the epithet applied to those sublime summits by a French lady in her company. "She was much impressed and

[17] Tacitus, *Agricola,* ch. xxv. (Maurice Hutton).
[18] Swinburne, *The Triumph of Time.*
[19] Shelley, *Passage of the Apennines.*

rather nervous."[20] Such an attitude is, of course, much more familiar to us in connection with places more remote. Thus Pierre Loti, writing in September 1871, says of Tierra del Fuego: "This nature which nothing animates is peculiarly sinister of aspect during the somber days of winter. The solitude and the profound silence which reign all about oppress one's heart."

I heartily agree with Tenney Frank[21] in his appreciation of Catullus as a lover of the mountains, for Catullus, and also Lucretius, Virgil, and Horace — if we read them aright — furnish quite sufficient evidence that, notwithstanding their less favorable environment, these great poets were deeply appreciative of the grandeur of mountain scenery. As for later Romans, let us remember to their credit that mountain climbing for other than military purposes was not unknown. Seneca, for instance, was so desirous of learning whether Mount Aetna was dwindling in size that he asked his friend Lucilius, the procurator of Sicily, to make the ascent. One of the emperors, too,

20 Mary King Waddington, *Italian Letters of a Diplomat's Wife*, New York, 1917, p. 13.

21 Tenney Frank, *Catullus and Horace*, p. 47. See p. 201 above.

actually qualified for membership in a modern Alpine Club. His biographers tell us that Hadrian climbed at least three mountains — Theches in Pontus, from which the Ten Thousand first saw the Black Sea, Casius in Syria, and Aetna in Sicily. His geographical range was wide, and his motive — at least with Casius and Aetna — an aesthetic one. He wanted to see the sun rise![22] It would not do to apply here the principle *ab uno disce omnes,* but we may well believe that, if an emperor could do such a deed, it was no uncommon feat among his subjects.

[22] For these and other instances of mountain climbing in antiquity, see H. F. Tozer, *Ancient Geography,* Cambridge, England, 1897, and W. W. Hyde, "The Mountains of Greece," in *The Bulletin of the Geographical Society of Philadelphia,* XIII. 1915, and Hyde's "Ancient Appreciation of Mountain Scenery." (Cf. n. 12.)

BIBLIOGRAPHY

BIBLIOGRAPHY

ALLEN, GRANT, *The Attis of Catullus*. London, 1892.

ALLEN, K., *Treatment of Nature in the Poetry of the Roman Republic*. Madison, Wis., 1899.

BATT, MAX, *The Treatment of Nature in German Literature*. Chicago, 1902.

BIESE, ALFRED, *Die Entwicklung des Naturgefühls bei den Griechen und Römern*. 2 vols. Kiel, 1882–84.

BUTCHER, S. H., *Some Aspects of the Greek Genius*.[3] London and New York, 1904.

CARPENTER, RHYS, *The Esthetic Basis of Greek Art*. Bryn Mawr, Pa., 1921.

DICKINSON, G. LOWES, *The Greek View of Life*. London, 1904.

DUFF, J. WIGHT, *A Literary History of Rome*. New York, 1909.

FAIRCLOUGH, H. R., *The Classics and Our Twentieth-Century Poets*. Stanford University, 1927.

——, *The Attitude of the Greek Tragedians toward Nature*. Toronto, 1897.

GAYLEY, C. M., *The Classic Myths in English Literature and in Art*. Boston, 1911.

GEIKIE, SIR A., *The Love of Nature Among the Romans*. London, 1912.

HAIGHT, E. H., *Horace and his Art of Enjoyment*. New York, 1925.

HARDIE, W. R., *Lectures on Classical Subjects*. London, 1903. Chapter on "Feeling for Nature in the Greek and Roman Poets."

HARRISON, J. E., *Mythology*, in the "Our Debt to Greece and Rome" Series. New York, 1924.

——, *Mythology and Monuments of Ancient Athens*. London and New York, 1890.

JEBB, R. C., *The Growth and Influence of Classical Greek Poetry*. London, 1893.

KERLIN, R. T., *Theocritus, in English Literature*. Lynchburg, Va., 1910.

MACKAIL, JOHN WILLIAM, *Latin Literature*.[4] London, 1902.

MARTINENGO-CESARESCO, EVELYN, *The Outdoor Life in Greek and Roman Poets*. London and New York, 1911.

MURRAY, GILBERT, *Four Stages of Greek Religion*. New York, 1912.

PALGRAVE, F. T., *Landscape in Poetry*, from Homer to Tennyson. London, 1897.

ROBINSON, DAVID M., *Sappho and Her Influence*, in the "Our Debt to Greece and Rome" Series. New York, 1924.

ROBINSON, DAVID M., and MILLER, M. M., *The Songs of Sappho*. Lexington, Ky., 1925.

RUSKIN, JOHN, *The Works of*. London, 1872–80.

SARGEAUNT, JOHN, *The Trees, Shrubs, and Plants of Virgil*. Oxford, 1920.

SELLAR, W. Y., *The Roman Poets of the Republic*.[3] Oxford, 1889.

——, *The Roman Poets of the Augustan Age. Virgil*. Oxford, 1877; *Horace, and the Élegiac Poets*. Oxford, 1892.

SHAIRP, J. C., *On Poetic Interpretation of Nature*. Boston, 1896.

SIKES, E. E., *Roman Poetry*. London and New York, 1923. Chapter on "Nature in Latin Poets."

STRONG, E. S., *Roman Sculpture from Augustus to Constantine*. London, 1907.

SYMONDS, JOHN ADDINGTON, *Studies of the Greek Poets*. London, 1877 and 1879.

TOZER, H. F., *Geography of Greece*. London, 1873.

WALDSTEIN, CHARLES, *Essays on the Art of Pheidias*. Cambridge, England, and New York, 1885.

WRIGHT, W. C., *A Short History of Greek Literature*. New York, 1907.

ZIELINSKI, F. F., *The Religion of Ancient Greece*. Trans. by G. R. Noyes. London, 1926.

Our Debt to Greece and Rome

AUTHORS AND TITLES

HOMER. *John A. Scott.*
SAPPHO. *David M. Robinson.*
EURIPIDES. *F. L. Lucas.*
ARISTOPHANES. *Louis E. Lord.*
DEMOSTHENES. *Charles D. Adams.*
THE POETICS OF ARISTOTLE. *Lane Cooper.*
GREEK RHETORIC AND LITERARY CRITICISM. *W. Rhys Roberts.*
LUCIAN. *Francis G. Allinson.*
CICERO AND HIS INFLUENCE. *John C. Rolfe.*
CATULLUS. *Karl P. Harrington.*
LUCRETIUS AND HIS INFLUENCE. *George Depue Hadzsits.*
OVID. *Edward Kennard Rand.*
HORACE. *Grant Showerman.*
VIRGIL. *John William Mackail.*
SENECA THE PHILOSOPHER. *Richard Mott Gummere.*
APULEIUS. *Elizabeth Hazelton Haight.*
MARTIAL. *Paul Nixon.*
PLATONISM. *Alfred Edward Taylor.*
ARISTOTELIANISM. *John L. Stocks.*
STOICISM. *Robert Mark Wenley.*
LANGUAGE AND PHILOLOGY. *Roland G. Kent.*

AUTHORS AND TITLES

Aeschylus and Sophocles. *J. T. Sheppard.*

Greek Religion. *Walter Woodburn Hyde.*

Survivals of Roman Religion. *Gordon J. Laing.*

Mythology. *Jane Ellen Harrison.*

Ancient Beliefs in The Immortality of The Soul. *Clifford H. Moore.*

Stage Antiquities. *James Turney Allen.*

Plautus and Terence. *Gilbert Norwood.*

Roman Politics. *Frank Frost Abbott.*

Psychology, Ancient and Modern. *G. S. Brett.*

Ancient and Modern Rome. *Rodolfo Lanciani.*

Warfare by Land and Sea. *Eugene S. McCartney.*

The Greek Fathers. *James Marshall Campbell.*

Greek Biology and Medicine. *Henry Osborn Taylor.*

Mathematics. *David Eugene Smith.*

Love of Nature among the Greeks and Romans. *H. R. Fairclough.*

Ancient Writing and its Influence. *B. L. Ullman.*

Greek Art. *Arthur Fairbanks.*

Architecture. *Alfred M. Brooks.*

Engineering. *Alexander P. Gest.*

Modern Traits in Old Greek Life. *Charles Burton Gulick.*

Roman Private Life. *Walton Brooks McDaniel.*

Greek and Roman Folklore. *William Reginald Halliday.*

Ancient Education. *J. F. Dobson.*